CW01672971

FIRST PRINTING 1992

PRINCE OF WALES AND FAMILY (1991)
Prince Charles enjoys a relaxing moment with Princess Diana, Prince William and Prince Henry (standing)

Camera Press
Austral-International

The People's Prince

A collection of major addresses
by His Royal Highness
Prince Charles,
Prince of Wales.

Published for
THE AUSTRALIAN HERITAGE SOCIETY
P.O. Box 7409. Cloisters Square, Perth Western Australia 6850
by
VERITAS PUBLISHING COMPANY PTY. LTD.
A.C.N. 008 931 619
P.O. Box 42, Cranbrook, Western Australia 6321.

ISBN 0-646-09389-4

INTRODUCTION

In September 1977, the Australian Heritage Society published a complete record of Christmas messages to the Commonwealth, from 1952 to 1976, given by Her Majesty Queen Elizabeth the Second. The publication also included Her Majesty's Silver Jubilee address.

The Australian Heritage Society now proudly offers a selection of major addresses by His Royal Highness Prince Charles, with a Foreword by one of Australia's most distinguished Ambassadors, Sir Walter Crocker, former Lieutenant-Governor of South Australia.

Prince Charles shows true leadership, in the sense that while he always speaks with modesty and good humour, he dares to articulate what the great majority of ordinary people feel about such things as the ugliness of modern architecture and modern art. With his genuine love and understanding of that great English genius, William Shakespeare, the Prince reveals a deeper insight into the human drama than most of the political figures who seek to strut the world stage today.

He touched many sensitive nerves when he criticised the failure of modern education to instil among the young a love and understanding of the priceless English language which enables a people to understand and value their own cultural heritage. He draws a sweeping picture of how, in the break-up of the Soviet Empire, peoples of different ethnic and cultural backgrounds, are seeking to go back to their roots, and urges that any people who wish to survive into the future should tap back into their roots.

It was something of a surprise to the Australian Heritage Society to discover that although the Prince's speeches were very much in the public domain, not one of the Publishing Houses had taken it upon itself to publish them, seemingly allowing the speeches to 'gather dust' among the files.

In making available this collection of major addresses by Prince Charles, the Australian Heritage Society believes that a more general reading and study of them will encourage the reader to 'drink the sap' of his own cultural heritage.

In speaking so ably and courageously for that great majority whose instincts and feelings are ignored by the materially powerful and the pseudo-intellectuals, well might Prince Charles become known as "The People's Prince".

Betty Luks (Editor)
Heritage.

FOREWORD

Existence for living things on earth carries no guarantee of permanence, as the fate of diprotodons and mastodons reminds us. Still less is there a guarantee that the high standards of living, by far the highest ever known, now enjoyed by humanity in the developed countries for a century, is permanent. For them and their inhabitants the rule of the survival of the fittest has been suspended. The suspension has been made possible by the advance of knowledge and practice in physics, chemistry and the biological sciences, in medicine, in engineering, and in the scientific knowledge of human behaviour, and particularly by combining these advances with the Welfare State.

But now not only the Third World (which has not been untouched by the advances) but the whole world, and particularly the developed countries, face stresses which could entail calamities comparable with those of the Black Death in the Middle Ages. We have recently been hearing a little but soon will be hearing much more about the degradation of soil and plant cover, genetic diversity, forest destruction and the effects of over-population, and of polluting the earth's air and waters. Even the climates of the earth are under threat. And new viruses threaten the food supply and foreshadow new diseases; AIDS is one grim reminder.

The threats are compounded by instabilities, brought about by human greed and human folly -- in the financial system (which is fiduciary and fragile) and in the system of international relations. (The vacuum left in Africa and parts of Asia through the hasty termination of the British, the French, and the other European empires has been filled largely by military, or quasi-military, dictatorships as corrupt and violent as they are incompetent; Saddam Hussein, Idi Amin, Gaddafi are prototypes not exceptions. The United Nations, of an unprecedented size, costliness and futility, has cumbered the scene by institutionalizing myths, stereotypes and fads, especially about equality and what purports to be human rights, and has brought little to peace but much to confusion.) TV and the mass media as a whole, but particularly TV and the practice of treating news as a branch of entertainment, goes on softening intelligence and rationality at large.

With this has gone a softening of the moral base world-wide but notably in the developed countries. Crime, violence (now an average of three murders a day in some American cities), vandalism, arson, drugs, hedonism, and dishonesty all the way up, and blatant, from plumbers and electricians to the learned professions and to top levels of industry, finance and public life, are now commonplace in the developed countries. Is humanity becoming ungovernable?

It is against this background of contemporary realities that the addresses of the Prince of Wales are to be read and welcomed. He is concerned not with the fashionable or the merely immediate but with realities of emphatic importance. Ranging over a period of ten years, from 1982 to 1991, his addresses deal with such subjects as the environment, town planning and architecture, housing for the poor, treatment of the mentally sick and the disabled, the bases of education, the teaching of English, the heritage of our great literature (he talks in particular about Shakespeare, the King James Version of the Bible, and the Cranmer and 1661 versions of The Book of Common Prayer), and the place of tradition and continuity in cultures of quality. He is mindful too of the role of religion.

The addresses are patently sincere and from the heart. They are free of censoriousness or cocksureness and are marked by modesty (he describes himself as a late-developer) and courtesy as much as by relevance and balance. What he says is buttressed with reading and reflection. And it is pervaded by the sense that life is a gift and a gift well worth having but that if humanity is to keep and enjoy the gift it will have to do better than at present.

Here and there his pleas would have gained had he suggested, or enlarged on, courses for practical action though of course it would be absurd to expect a blue print. His courage is such that he takes on such saints of modernity as the painter Francis Bacon, the town planner Lord Holford, the architects for whom "every building must be vertical, straight, unbending, only at right angles", the destructive philistine developers, and the education people who exclude Shakespeare and other imperishable classics from pupils and students in order to foist on them the "relevant" modernist trash in vogue. There is nothing from him on those ultimate molochs of our culture -- TV and pop music. Not yet. Perhaps later he will take them on. His grasp and his courage are equal to that too.

His courage is as notable as the variety and quality of his other skills -- sailing, horsemanship, piloting planes, farming (including organic), music and painting in addition to a considerable list of serious reading.

The Australian Heritage Society is to be commended for making these refreshing addresses from the heir to the throne available to the public.

Walter Crocker*

---

* Lieut.-Governor of South Australia, 1973-1982
Ambassador of Australia, 1951-1970

By concentrating on smaller and smaller fragments of the body modern medicine perhaps loses sight of the patient as a whole human being, and by reducing health to mechanical functioning it is no longer able to deal with the phenomenon of healing. ... The term "healer" is viewed with suspicion and the concepts of health and healing are probably not generally discussed enough in medical schools. But to reincorporate the notion of healing into the practice of medicine does not necessarily mean that medical science will have to be less scientific.

SPEECH GIVEN BY H.R.H. THE PRINCE OF WALES AT THE BRITISH MEDICAL ASSOCIATION

Tuesday, 14th December, 1982

I HAVE often thought that one of the less attractive traits of various professional bodies and institutions is the deeply ingrained suspicion and outright hostility which can exist towards anything unorthodox or unconventional. I suppose it is inevitable that something which is different should arouse strong feelings on the part of the majority whose conventional wisdom is being challenged or, in a more social sense, whose way of life and customs are being insulted by something rather alien. I suppose, too, that human nature is such that we are frequently prevented from seeing that what is taken for today's unorthodoxy is probably going to be tomorrow's convention. Perhaps we just have to accept it is God's will that the unorthodox individual is doomed to years of frustration, ridicule and failure in order to act out his role in the scheme of things, until his day arrives and mankind is ready to receive his message; a message which he probably finds hard to explain himself, but which he knows comes from a far deeper source than conscious thought.

The renowned 16th-century healer, Paracelsus, was just such an individual. He is probably remembered more for his fight against orthodoxy than for his achievements in the medical field. As a result of his unorthodox approach to medicine in his time he was equated with the damnable Dr. Faustus. Of the barbers, surgeons and pharmacists he complained that "they begrudge the honour I won healing Princes and noblemen and they say my powers come from the devil". And yet in his day and age he was operating as a one-man B.M.A. (British Medical Association), criticizing the abuse amongst pharmacists and attacking the quack remedies -- vipers' blood, "mummy" powder, unicorn horn and so on. In 1527, by an act of which I am sure today's younger doctors would be proud, he burnt the famous textbook of medieval medicine, the Canon of Avicenna, which became a symbol of rebellion against pedantry and unthinking acceptance of ancient doctrines.

But what kind of man was Paracelsus? A charlatan or a gifted healer? In my view he was far from being a charlatan. In this, the 150th anniversary year of the B.M.A., we could do worse than to look again briefly at the principles he so desperately believed in, for they have a message for our time -- a time in which science has tended to become estranged from Nature. That is the moment when we should remember Paracelsus. Above all, he maintained that there were four pillars on which the whole art of healing rested. The first was philosophy; the second, astronomy (or what we might now call psychology); the third, alchemy (or biochemistry) and the fourth virtue (in other words, the professional skill of the doctor). He then went on to outline the basic qualifications for a doctor: "... like each plant and metallic remedy, the doctor, too, must have a specific virtue. He must be intimate with Nature. He must have the intuition which is necessary to understand the patient, his body, his disease. He must have the 'feel' and the 'touch' which make it possible for him to be in sympathetic communication with the patient's spirits." Paracelsus believed that the good doctor's therapeutic success largely depends on his ability to inspire the patient with confidence and to mobilize his will to health. By the way, he also recommended chastity and fasting to heighten diagnostic sensitiveness and to intensify one's hypnotic power!

I know that there are a considerable number of doctors who operate by these kinds of basic principles, because several have written to me, but nevertheless the modern science of medicine still tends to be based, as George Engel writes, "... on the notion of the body as a machine, of disease as the consequence of breakdown of the machine, and of the doctor's task as repair of the machine." By concentrating on smaller and smaller fragments of the body modern medicine perhaps loses sight of the patient as a whole human being, and by reducing health to mechanical functioning it is no longer able to deal with the phenomenon of healing. And here I come back to my original point. The term "healer" is viewed with suspicion and the concepts of health and healing are probably not generally discussed enough in medical schools. But to reincorporate the notion of healing into the practice of medicine does not necessarily mean that medical science will have to be less scientific. Through the centuries healing has been practised by folk-healers who are guided by traditional wisdom that sees illness as a disorder of the whole person, involving not only the patient's body, but his mind, his self-image, his dependence on the physical and social environment, as well as his relation to the cosmos. Paracelsus constantly repeated the old adage that "Nature heals, the doctor nurses" -- and it is well to remember that these sorts of healers still treat the majority of patients throughout the world. Some of them, in the form of black Christian bishops in Africa, are subjected to the most appalling kind of mis-informed abuse and censure, which so characterized the worst elements of missionary activity amongst populations whose childlike acceptance of the symbols of life and of Nature is one of their most endearing and vital qualities.

I would suggest that the whole imposing edifice of modern medicine, for all its breath-taking successes is, like the celebrated Tower of Pisa, slightly off balance. Of course no one could be stupid enough to deny the enormous benefits which the advances of medical science in this century have conferred upon us all. To take only one example -- penicillin administered in a case of infective heart disease leads to survival in an illness otherwise uniformly fatal. Anyone who has had this kind of experience is likely to be a powerful supporter of modern methods in medicine, but nevertheless the fact remains that contemporary medicine as a whole tends to be fascinated by the objective, statistical, computerized approach to the healing of the sick. If disease is regarded as an objective problem isolated from all personal factors, then surgery plus more and more powerful drugs must be the answer. Already the cost of drugs supplied to patients by the N.H.S. (National Health Service) alone is well over £2000 million a year. It is frightening how dependent upon drugs we are all becoming and how easy it is for doctors to prescribe them as the universal panacea for our ills. Wonderful as many of them are, it should still be more widely stressed by doctors that the health of human beings is so often determined by their behaviour, their food and the nature of their environment.

The last word on this subject remains with Paracelsus, whose name should be synonymous with the common health, which I have been asked to toast this evening. He hoped to show, above all, that the "light of Nature" was in the hearts of men, not in books. With all the conviction of a man who follows his inner voice, he made a desperate supplication -- "Would we humans knew our hearts in truth, nothing on earth would be impossible for us!"

Now, moreover, we are seeing the gradual expansion of housing co-operatives, particularly in the inner city areas of Liverpool, where the tenants are able to work with an architect of their own who listens to their comments and their ideas and tries to design the kind of environment they want, rather than the kind which tends to be imposed upon them without any degree of choice.

SPEECH GIVEN BY H.R.H. THE PRINCE OF WALES AT A ROYAL GALA EVENING TO CELEBRATE THE 150th ANNIVERSARY OF THE ROYAL INSTITUTE OF BRITISH ARCHITECTS

Hampton Court : 30th May, 1984.

Ladies and Gentlemen,

IT SEEMS entirely appropriate in this anniversary year that the Royal Institute of British Architects should nominate Mr. Charles Correa to the Queen to receive the Royal Gold Medal for Architecture. I have heard that he is a brilliant modern architect who has been responsible for splendidly brilliant and sensitive modern architecture, invariably of low cost. But it is his imaginative concern for those who suffer the disability of poverty in Bombay and the third world generally that he is justly famous. It is for this as well as his supreme skill as an architect that he is being honoured this evening.

It would seem that sesquicentenarics arc coming thick and fast nowadays. Last year I was invited to become President of the British Medical Association for its 150th anniversary and greatly enjoyed holding that particular office. I am enormously relieved, I must say, that you have not asked me to be President of the R.I.B.A. (Royal Institute of British Architects) this year because while it is comparatively easy to be a practising hypochondriac it is probably much more difficult to become the architectural equivalent. On the other hand, my great-great-great grandfather, The Prince Consort, indulged himself whole-heartedly in a kind of architectural hypochondria as often as he could. Osborne and Balmoral are, of course, the most obvious examples of his personal involvement with the design of buildings but he also busied himself with the design of farm buildings and the interiors of houses. No detail seemed to be so small as to escape his attention and, as a result, we have been left with a series of buildings which never fail to fascinate and which display great individuality (although always inspired originally by some earlier style of architecture). Embellishment appears to have been a vital ingredient, as far as Prince Albert was concerned, to any building and the more symbolic it was, the better. I sometimes can't help wondering whether planning permission would be forthcoming nowadays for some of his designs, but perhaps with the present, welcome reaction to the modern movement, which seems to be taking place in our society, it **would** be forthcoming. For at last people are beginning to see that it is possible, and important in human terms, to respect old buildings, street plans and traditional scales and at the same time not to feel guilty about a preference for façades, ornaments and soft materials. At last, after witnessing the wholesale destruction of Georgian and Victorian housing in most of our cities, people have begun to realize that it **is** possible to restore old buildings and, what is more, that there are architects willing to undertake such projects.

For far too long, it seems to me, some planners and architects have consistently ignored the feelings and wishes of the mass of ordinary people in this country. Perhaps, when you think about it, it is hardly surprising as architects tend to have been trained to design buildings from scratch -- to tear down and rebuild. Except in Interior Design courses, students are not taught to rehabilitate, nor do they ever meet the ultimate users of buildings in their training -- indeed, they can often go through their whole career without doing so. Consequently a large number of us have developed a feeling that architects tend to design houses for the approval of fellow architects and critics, not for the tenants. The same feelings, by the way, have been shared by disabled people who consider that with a little extra thought, consultation and planning, their already difficult lives could be made that much less complicated. Having said that, I am told that the Department of the Environment is preparing an amendment to the Building Regulations which will mean that in future, buildings will have to be designed so that they are accessible, which in turn will make it easier for architects who are working for clients. This is excellent news and could ultimately transform the lives of over two million people throughout the country. I want to take this opportunity too, to express my gratitude to the President of the R.I.B.A. for his willingness to join with a group of architects, planners, government officials, journalists and disabled people who came to lunch with me in March to discuss this very problem. I would also like to say how impressed I am to see how the

R.I.B.A. has overcome the difficulty of access to their headquarters in London by means of an ingenious combination of steps and ramp. I know that many architects are now fully aware of the needs of disabled people and of their understandable desire to live as near 'normal' a life as possible. Because of this increasing awareness on the part of architects and planners I am sure that there will be considerable progress in this field. But there is a particular problem to overcome and that is the fire regulations which apply to all public buildings. Selwyn Goldsmith wrote about this in his *Designing for the Disabled*, which the R.I.B.A. helped initiate in 1961. Referring to building hazards to disabled people and the demands that exist for strict controls, he says, "For those who administer fire regulations the easy way out is always to say, 'Yes, we must impose more controls because we are bothered about people dying.' The more difficult alternative is to say, 'No, we shall not, because we are concerned about people living.' "

To be concerned about the way people live, about the environment they inhabit, and the kind of community that is created by that environment, should surely be one of the prime requirements of a really good architect. It has been most encouraging to see the development of Community Architecture as a natural reaction to the policy of decamping people to new towns and overspill estates where the extended family patterns of support were destroyed and the community life was lost. Now, moreover, we are seeing the gradual expansion of housing co-operatives, particularly in the inner city areas of Liverpool, where the tenants are able to work with an architect of their own who listens to their comments and their ideas and tries to design the kind of environment they want, rather than the kind which tends to be imposed upon them without any degree of choice.

This sort of development, spear-headed as it is by such individuals as a Vice-President of the R.I.B.A., Rod Hackney, and Ted Cullinan -- a man after my own heart, as he believes strongly that the architect must produce something that is visually beautiful as well as socially useful -- offers something very promising in terms of inner city renewal and urban housing, not to mention community garden design. Enabling the client community to be involved in the detailed process of design rather than exclusively the local authority, is, I am sure, the kind of development we should be examining more closely. Apart from anything else, there is an assumption that if people have played a part in creating something they might conceivably treat it as their own possession and look after it, thus making an attempt at reducing the problem of vandalism.

What I believe is important about community architecture is that it has shown 'ordinary' people that their views are worth having; that architects and planners do not necessarily have the monopoly of knowing best about taste, style and planning; that they need not be made to feel guilty or ignorant if their natural preference is for the more 'traditional' designs -- for a small garden, for courtyards, arches and porches -- and that there is a growing number of architects prepared to listen and to offer imaginative ideas.

On that note I can't help thinking how much more worthwhile it would be if a community approach could have been used in the Mansion House Square project. It would be a tragedy if the character and skyline of our capital city were to be further ruined and St. Paul's dwarfed by yet another giant glass stump, better suited to down-town Chicago than the City of London. It is hard to imagine that London before the last war must have had one of the most beautiful sky lines of any great city, if those who recall it are to be believed. Those who do, say that the affinity between buildings and the earth, in spite of the city's immense size, was so close and organic that the houses looked almost as though they had grown out of the earth and had not been imposed upon it -- grown moreover, in such a way that as few trees as possible were thrust out of the way. Those who knew it then and loved it, as so many British love Venice without concrete stumps and glass towers, and those who can imagine what it was like, must associate with the sentiments in one of Aldous Huxley's earliest and most successful novels, *Antic Hay*, where the main character, an unsuccessful architect reveals a model of London as Christopher Wren wanted to rebuild it after the Great Fire and describes how Wren was so obsessed with the opportunity the fire gave the city to rebuild itself into a greater and more glorious vision. What, then, are we doing to our capital city now? What have we done to it since the bombing during the war? What are we shortly going to do to one of its most famous areas -- Trafalgar Square? Instead of designing an extension to the elegant façade of the National Gallery which complements it and continues the concept of columns and domes, it looks as if we may be presented with a kind of vast municipal fire station, complete with the sort of tower that contains the siren. I would understand better this type of high tech approach if you demolished the whole of Trafalgar Square and started again with a single architect responsible for the entire layout, but what is proposed is like a monstrous carbuncle on the face of a much loved and elegant friend. Apart from anything else, it defeats me why anyone wishing to display the early Renaissance pictures belonging to the gallery should do so in a new gallery so manifestly at odds with the whole spirit of that age of astonishing proportion.

Why can't we have those curves and arches that express feeling in design? What is wrong with them? Why has everything got to be vertical, straight, unbending, only at right angles -- and functional? As if the National Gallery extension wasn't enough, they are now apparently planning to redevelop the large, oval-bellied 19th-century building, known as the Grand Hotel, which stands on the south-west corner of Trafalgar Square and which was saved from demolition in 1974 after a campaign to rescue it. As with the National Gallery, I believe, the plan is to put this redevelopment out to competition, in which case we can only criticize the judges and not the architects, for I suspect there will be some entries representative of the present-day school of Romantic Pragmatism, which could at least provide an alternative. Goethe once said, "There is nothing more dreadful than imagination without taste." In this 150th anniversary year, which provides an opportunity for a fresh look at the path ahead and in which by now you are probably regretting having asked me to take part, may I express the earnest hope that the next 150 years will see a new harmony between imagination and taste and in the relationship between the architects and the people of this country.

Not only did they wreck the London skyline in general. They all did their best to lose the great dome in a jostling scrum of office buildings, so mediocre that the only way you ever remember them is by the frustration they induce -- like a basketball team standing shoulder-to-shoulder between you and the Mona Lisa.

SPEECH GIVEN BY H.R.H. THE PRINCE OF WALES AT THE CORPORATION OF LONDON PLANNING AND COMMUNICATION COMMITTEE'S ANNUAL DINNER

The Mansion House : Tuesday, 1st December, 1987

My Lord Mayor, Mr. Chairman, My Lords, Ladies and Gentlemen,

IT IS an honour for all of us, My Lord Mayor, to be in this magnificent room. We are often struck by the splendour in which the City houses its first citizen and the generous surroundings in which it entertains its guests, coming as I do from the more modest surroundings of Kensington Palace -- the servants' quarters, to be exact.

But I know, My Lord Mayor, that all this splendour is not just for you, but expresses the commercial triumphs and the benevolence of the entire City of London.

Last year, your Guest of Honour at this dinner was a Minister from the Department of the Environment, Mr. William Waldegrave, who urged the City of London to continue to celebrate its commercial success by commissioning more wonderful buildings. Mr. Cassidy has spoken of your achievements since then and, despite your recent setback, you have still accomplished the feat of adding an additional six million square feet of offices to the Square Mile.

But that raises a problem, and it is this: How to create commercial architecture as effective as the Mansion House, or the Royal Exchange or Sir Edwin Lutyens' pre-war Midland Bank -- worthy celebrations, I would have said, of the fruits of commerce. Can anyone in this room really claim that Bucklersbury House, the Stock Exchange Tower or Paternoster Square are creditable successors to those earlier buildings?

And it is not just **me** who is complaining -- countless people are appalled by what has happened to their capital city, but feel totally powerless to do anything about it.

Nowhere is the problem more acute than in that special area around St. Paul's Cathedral. What **have we done**, Ladies and Gentlemen, to St. Paul's? What are we about to do to it now? Why in fact does St. Paul's matter so much? Because it is our greatest national monument. It has been the scene of the funerals on an heroic scale of Nelson and Wellington, and I well remember the cold March morning when Sir Winston Churchill followed them into that great sacred building.

On the terrible night of December 29th 1940, when the surroundings of the cathedral were devastated and an incendiary bomb lodged in the outer dome, it was Mr. Churchill himself who had despatched the message to the Guildhall: "St. Paul's must be saved at all costs." The dramatic photograph of the great black dome standing out against the swirling smoke and flames is something that most of us today know about.

Then it gave new meaning to the cathedral as a symbol of faith and a monument to Britain's resolve. **Now** it reminds us of the place St. Paul's occupies at the very heart of our nation as the spiritual centre of the capital city.

St. Paul's is not just a symbol and a mausoleum for national heroes. It is also a temple which glorifies God through the inspired expression of man's craftsmanship and art. Architecturally, I believe it has a character all of its own:

That familiar dome, raised high on its balustraded drum, often appearing with a ghostly magnificence through the London mists and river fogs. That skyline with the sentinel towers at its west end and the chorus of spires of a hundred parish churches which Canaletto painted in the eighteenth century, was without doubt one of the architectural wonders of the world, the equal in architecture to Shakespeare's plays.

What, then, **have** we done to it since the bombing? In the space of a mere fifteen years, in the sixties and seventies, and in spite of all sorts of elaborate rules **supposedly** designed to protect that great view, your predecessors, as the planners, architects and developers of the City, wrecked the London skyline and desecrated the dome of St. Paul's.

Not only did they wreck the London skyline in general, they all did their best to lose the great dome in a jostling scrum of office buildings, so mediocre that the only way you ever remember them is by the frustration they induce -- like a basketball team standing shoulder-to-shoulder between you and the Mona Lisa. In Paris, the French have built some pretty awful tower blocks in La Défense, but can you really imagine them building those same towers around Notre Dame? Can you imagine the Italians walling in St. Mark's in Venice or St. Peter's in Rome with office blocks the size of the Pirelli building in Milan? You can't. But we've done something almost as bad, and we've done it to ourselves.

And at street level, just look at Paternoster Square! Did modern planners and architects in London ever use their eyes? Those planners swept away the lanes and alleys, hidden-away squares and courtyards which in most other European countries would have been lovingly rebuilt after the War. I was in Germany a few weeks ago, and returned greatly impressed by the way in which Munich has been so carefully restored after the ravages of the war.

In devastated Warsaw, they used the paintings of Canaletto's nephew, Bellotto, as blue-prints so that they could recreate the intimacy of the lost city. Lost, but found again; they brought it back from the dead. **We** buried the dead deeper. What did we do? Here, even the street where Shakespeare and Milton brought their manuscripts, the legendary Paternoster Row, 'The Row', the very heart of publishing since Elizabethan times, was turned into a concrete service road leading to an underground carpark!

You have, Ladies and Gentlemen, to give this much to the Luftwaffe: When it knocked down our buildings, it didn't replace them with anything more offensive than rubble. **We** did that. Clausewitz called war the continuation of diplomacy by other means. Around St. Paul's, planning turned out to be the continuation of war by other means.

What then went wrong? Your predecessors bought the fashionable post-war orthodoxy that arose from the 1947 **Town and Country Planning Act** and the Ministry guidelines, only too appropriately entitled 'The Redevelopment of Central Areas'. The author was Lord Holford, whom the City appointed as their Planning Consultant, the man responsible for today's Paternoster Square. St. Paul's, in their jargon, was no doubt just a 'worship unit'.

What your predecessors wanted was scientifically conceived slabs, permanently bathed in sunlight for the people at work in the offices. We all know how that particular dream turned out! It might be said that Paternoster Square, if it gave us nothing else, gave us space to play in. Unfortunately, nothing but the wind plays there. I am told that, on a sunny day, it is possible to sit down, if you buy a drink from the pub first, and hurry to bag a share of the only bench. I was told that by a survivor...

Paternoster was one of the very first of these C.D.A's. -- Comprehensive Development Areas. Praised by architects, it became the model for schemes that have destroyed the city centres of Bristol, Newcastle, Birmingham, Worcester -- the list is endless. 'The Rape of Britain', it has been called.

Fortunately, Ladies and Gentlemen, today, we have a second chance. As a result of technological change, places like Paternoster are obsolete. Here, surely, is a heaven-sent opportunity to build a model of real quality, of excellence, next to so great a building, in the heart of our capital city. I, for one, would love to see the London skyline restored, and I am sure I am not alone in feeling this. If we wanted, we could use this 'second chance' to rebuild a 'City Without Towers'. So why don't we set that as a goal for the millenium year 2000?

Now, I seem to have acquired something of a reputation, in certain quarters, for my interventions in architectural matters. I believe I have been accused of setting myself up as a new, undemocratic hurdle in the planning process -- a process we are supposed to leave to the professionals. But the professionals have been doing it their way, thanks to the planning legislation, for the last forty years. We, poor mortals, are forced to live in the shadow of their achievements. Everywhere I go, it's one of the things people complain about most and, if there is one message I would like to deliver this evening, in no uncertain terms, it is that large numbers of us in this country are fed up with being talked down to and dictated to by the existing planning, architectural and development establishment.

But to return to Paternoster. And I do so because it is an area of such vital importance to our city that it is worth taking up a position on it and raising my standard over it. The fact is that the Project Director, Mr. Lipton, kindly invited me, in private, to comment on the seven finalists in the private competition to choose a new Master Plan for the area. I agreed and, I have to say, was deeply depressed that none of them had risen to the occasion.

What demoralized me? First, the Competition Brief, whose "overriding commercial consideration (without which the Paternoster Square project will not be built)" -- and I am now quoting from the document itself -- "is to provide as much office space [they want one million square feet, Ladies and Gentlemen!] of the highest quality and efficiency, as is possible within the planning constraints" -- that, and what is called a "bold concept for retailing". A bold concept for retailing! What a challenge! I suppose Sir Christopher Wren was inspired by the same sort of brief. "Give us a bold concept for worship, Sir Christopher -- and the most efficient praying area within the planning constraints."

With such a brief, what alternative was there for the competitors, all of them world-famous architects, than to cram in as much as possible on to the site? None of them, I believe, addressed the primary problems of appropriateness and architectural good manners; none gave sufficient attention to the materials to be used, nor even considered which style of architecture would be appropriate. Surely such eminent architects should have questioned the brief?

Surely here, if anywhere, was the time and place to sacrifice some profit, if need be, for generosity of vision, for elegance, for dignity; for buildings which would raise our spirits and our faith in commercial enterprise and prove that capitalism can have a human face, instead of that of a robot or word processor. On such a site, market forces, I would suggest, are not enough.

This brings me to another question: What place, if any, do the opinions of the general public have within the legal labyrinth of the planning system (a subject to which Mr. Cassidy has just referred)? Should a private developer be allowed to set up a private competition for a site of such historic importance, about which the public have been kept in the dark -- and still are -- whose winner will eventually submit a single scheme to the City Planning Committee, which will have no option between accepting it or rejecting it?

If they reject it, the developer can then appeal to the Secretary of State. Suppose he calls for a Public Enquiry and then turns it down, another and yet another scheme can be produced to go through the same process until at last the opponents of the scheme are worn down by the length of the proceedings and the hideous expense of it all. This is happening on the Mappin and Webb site opposite the Mansion House. **And** in Winchester; **and** in Lancaster.

Is it right that the people, their elected representatives, the Secretary of State himself, can take no initiative of their own? Is it sensible that they can only react to developers' proposals? There must be something wrong with a system which involves public opinion at so late a stage that the only course left open to the public is to obstruct the development through whatever means the planning system allows.

If the planning system is to blame, if the rules are at fault, then why don't we change them? To be specific, here are three major shortcomings in our system:

First, control over the design of buildings next to major monuments is fuzzy and, in practice, unenforceable. Just listen to this: "In considering whether to grant planning permission for development which affects a listed building or its setting, and in considering whether to grant listed building consent for any work, the local planning authority or the Secretary of State, as the case may be, shall have special regard for the desirability of preserving the building or its setting ..."

Is anyone surprised that you can drive a coach-and-four through this piece of legislation? And because post-war Paternoster Square is not a conservation area, there is even less that the City Planning Committee can do to control the design of buildings within it. Mind you, even in conservation areas, the obligation is similarly ill-defined. So why don't you have restrictions upon any new building within five hundred yards of an historic monument? After all, that's what the French do.

Second, and closely related to this -- again a point to which Mr. Cassidy has referred -- the Department of the Environment does **not** encourage planning authorities to set firm aesthetic guidelines in development. As things stand, they are only justified in rejecting a proposal if it is absolutely hideous; anything merely ugly must be allowed to get through.

Surely, then, we can learn from other countries? In France, since the Malraux Act of 1962, they have had the concept of 'secteurs sauvegardés', a bit like our conservation areas, only with more muscle behind them. They even spell out what bricks and tiles you must use -- essential if the character of the area is to be maintained.

Third, that skyline, once the envy of other cities: Let's admit that the approach adopted for protecting it over the past forty years has simply not worked. The rules are too woolly. Indeed, the post-war planners **meant** them to be woolly in the interests of what they called flexibility.

So why don't we return to some form of statutory height limit, which served us well in the past, and continues to serve other great cities? And when buildings like Sudbury House in Paternoster Square and the Stock Exchange Tower become obsolete, they should be redeveloped in such a way as to restore the domination of St. Paul's -- and our famous skyline as well.

To sum up: Because there is this broad discretionary element in our planning legislation, as well as the absence of aesthetic control, architects and developers have the wrong kind of freedom -- the freedom to impose their caprice, which is a kind of tyranny. Competitions even encourage them to come up with the voguish innovations and fashionable novelties that appeal to nobody but other architects. One prominent architect recently confessed, airily and with no apparent sign of shame, that some of his own earlier buildings have ceased to interest even him, now that the thrill of creativity has worn off.

Well, what kind of creativity is that? To put up a building which other people have to live with, and leave them to live with it while you wander off saying you're tired of it, and then to put up another one which you will presumably get tired of too, leaving yet more people to live with the all-too-durable consequences of your passing fancy. There is a terrible fecklessness to all this, when grown men can get whole **towns** in the family way, pay nothing towards maintenance, and call it romance.

Mr. Cassidy has just said that we need "more planning" to make buildings pleasing as well as more efficient. Perhaps not more, but better. In short, then, isn't it time to change direction and set down a few sensible rules such as limits on the height of buildings, the materials to be used, the proportions of windows, even the appropriate style perhaps. Such rules gave us Georgian London, and still give the French a largely unspoilt centre to their capital city.

And so, what about Paternoster Square? I am told that the competition schemes were merely first thoughts. The winners are only now getting down to producing actual plans. We must use this breathing space to have a proper debate. Let there be an informative exhibition showing the area as it was, the plans of Wren, Hawksmoor and Lutyens, as well as the present plans. Then people could judge for themselves. Perhaps this would be an opportunity to try out some firm guidelines to govern the master plan. But **please**, let it not be based on "overriding commercial considerations" -- at least not in this part of the City.

I am sometimes accused by architects of always being negative, so here, for what it's worth, is my personal vision: It should be a beautiful area on a human scale, built at ground level not on top of car park square, with small shops and businesses at ground level -- above all to cater for the needs of, and to create something special for, the three million tourists who already visit St. Paul's each year. With the opening of the Channel Tunnel, that figure is expected to rise to seven or eight million.

So, I would like to see the mediaeval street plan of pre-war Paternoster reconstructed, not out of mere nostalgia, but to give meaning to surviving fragments like Amen Court and the Chapter House, now left like dispossessed refugees in an arid desert of God-forsaken buildings. I would like to see a roofscape that gives the impression that St. Paul's is floating above it like a great ship on the sea. I would also like to see the kinds of materials Wren might have used -- soft red brick and stone dressings perhaps, and the ornament and detail of classical architecture, but on a scale humble enough not to compete with the monumentality of St. Paul's.

I would like to see architects working with artists and craftsmen, showing that pleasure and delight are indeed returning to architecture after their long exile. And I am not alone in longing to regain those wonderful views of St. Paul's rising above the rooftops over its first entablature. Can we not learn from the age of Wren, that unique moment in our architectural history when the vernacular gothic and the classical were fused in a vigorously attractive style?

Do we still have to strive to be a stunted imitation of Manhattan?

Now some people, I know, will say that I am not living in the real world of Big Bang and twenty-four-hour financial dealing; that my guidelines would deter any developer from taking on Paternoster. Further, they will say that my thinking would drive business out of the City and into the hands of foreign competition. But good architecture of the kind I have described **is** good for business. Who, with any choice, wants to work in an environment like Victoria Street?

Businesses flock to the City from all over the world just because, in addition to superb efficiency and competitiveness, they can find a unique environmental character: The Wren churches, the livery halls, places like Amen Court and Wardrobe Court, surviving backwaters with their cellar bars and restaurants; attractions which New York and Tokyo cannot offer. To use the jargon: As a world financial centre, the City of London is user-friendly, to a unique degree. In plain English, business people like it. So why spit on your luck? Even the great free-market economists, like von Hayek and von Mises, recognize the importance of what they refer to as "psychological profits".

So why not capitalize on many people's desire for an environment of character and charm, which is also more conducive to productive work because the surroundings make you feel better? This is very much the age of the computer and the word-processor, but why on earth do we have to be surrounded by buildings that look like such machines?

Why cannot we recall the example of our forbears who took enormous trouble to ennoble their commercial buildings -- buildings like Sir John Soane's Bank of England. There are a number of younger architects who share this feeling, but they rarely win the larger commercial commissions because they are considered to lack the necessary experience. But surely everybody has to start somewhere?

I see no reason, then, why wealth should not finance beauty that is in harmony with tradition, today as in the past. People too easily forget that the London of Wren's time was the greatest trading empire the world had ever seen. Yet it was of such a splendour that the vista Canaletto painted surpassed ancient Rome and even rivalled that of his own native city of Venice, itself a centre of world trade, and one which knew so well how the fruits of commerce should be celebrated in the arts and architecture.

We **can** make choices about the surroundings in which we live and work. Prosperity and beauty need not exclude each other. If the rules of the planning game are wrong, our democracy enables us to change them. Many younger architects today welcome the idea that beauty must be based upon the observance of rules, which indeed encourages the right kind of creative freedom rather than inhibiting it. And many of our best developers and builders would welcome a situation in which they knew where they actually stood.

So this, Ladies and Gentlemen, is a good time to reassert a sense of vision and civilized values amidst all the excitement and commercialism of the city. Perhaps such a scheme as I have sketched for Paternoster would help to drag us out of the bind of the deep aesthetic idleness which has afflicted the post-war world. What an inspiration it would be for other towns and cities in repairing the wounds of post-war architecture and town planning.

The City, My Lord Mayor, has every reason to feel proud of its commercial achievements. You should express your confidence in the environment for which you have responsibility. We have this unexpected second chance. Pray God we don't waste it **this** time.

If English is spoken in Heaven (as the spread of English as a world language makes more likely each year) God undoubtedly employs Cranmer as his speech-writer. The angels of the lesser ministries probably use the language of the New English Bible and the Alternative Service Book for internal memos.

AT THE PRESENTATION OF THE THOMAS CRANMER SCHOOLS PRIZE

Tuesday, 19th December, 1989

I ACCEPTED thc invitation to be Patron of the Thomas Cranmer Schools Prize simply because I mind about what may loosely be referred to as our heritage. Some may say it is an exaggerated concern and, indeed, as I have discovered only too plainly, if you actually stand up and talk about the importance of our heritage and the lessons to be learned from our forbears you are at once accused of having a quaint nostalgia for a picturesque, irrelevant past. It has forced me to reflect on why there is such a fierce obsession about being 'modern'. The fear of being considered old-fashioned seems to be so all-powerful that the more eternal values and principles which run like a thread through the whole tapestry of human existence are abandoned under the false assumption that they restrict progress. Well, I'm **not** afraid of being considered old-fashioned which is why I am standing here at this lectern wearing a double-breasted suit and turn-ups to my trousers, ready to declaim the fact that I believe the Prayer Book is a glorious part of every English-speaker's heritage and, as such, ought to be a Grade I listed edifice!

Do you recall that wonderful passage of Alan Bennet in *The Old Country*?

> I imagine (he wrote) that when it comes to the next prayer book they won't write He, meaning Him with a capital h. God will be written in the lower case to banish any lurking feeling of inferiority his worshippers might feel.

I would have liked to begin with a ringing phrase from the King James version of the Bible:

"Hearken to my words."

But the New English Bible translates the phrase in less commanding terms:

"Give me a hearing."

It might seem more humble but it also sounds less poetic: and what we have to ask ourselves, it seems to me, is whether, by making the words less poetic, you really do make them more democratic. Isn't there something rather patronising about that whole assumption?

Possibly there **are** more people today who read less well than people in the past, although I doubt it. Most people then couldn't read at all. But supposing it were true, whoever decided that for people who aren't very good at reading the best things to read are those written by people who aren't very good at writing? Poetry is for everybody, even if it's only a few phrases. But banality is for nobody. It might be accessible to all, but so is a desert.

The Book of Common Prayer has been the spiritual resource of English and English-speaking people for four centuries. It is a book of prayer for the whole community, devised and composed so that it might satisfy everyone. Cranmer, like the translators of the King James Bible, looked to the past as well as the present when he set about this task at a time of reformation and change; he compiled his Prayer Book in a spirit of reconciliation. To some of his contemporaries it seemed too conservative, to others too radical, but it has survived changes in Church and State that would have destroyed a liturgy less sensitive to the profound human need for continuity and permanence. The language Cranmer employed in the Prayer Book was quite deliberately "not of an age, but for all time".

And so it has survived by passing into common speech. Words and phrases from this liturgy have become part of the heritage of the English language by continuous reiteration through centuries, in public worship and private devotion. In Church of England day schools pupils used to learn by heart the great Collects from the Prayer Book, a practice much despised by educationalists today. But that learning by heart, together with regular Church services where the Prayer Book was the only rite, had a genuine influence on the minds and imaginations of ordinary men and women. Though their own speech could not command the cadences and rhythms of Cranmer's prayers, because they were familiar with them they remembered them! At home, abroad, in hospitals, on battlefields, in solitude, in society, in trouble and in prosperity, these words were remembered and gave comfort and hope in the great crises of innumerable human lives.

The Book of Common Prayer reminds us of human frailty "among the sundry and manifold changes of the world" and, at the same time, of the consolation of "the means of grace and the hope of glory".

At this point it is perhaps worth recalling what George Orwell pointed out in '1984' "that the best way of getting rid of history and thought is to get rid of the language of history and ideas". So he invented 'Newspeak' for his nightmare communist world. Consider the following: "We do not presume to come to this Thy table, O merciful Lord, trusting in our own righteousness, but in Thy manifold and great mercies." Compare the courtesy of Cranmer's language with the crassness of *The Alternative Service Book* which spends much time telling the Deity what he must already know: "Lord Jesus Christ, only Son of the Father, Lord God, Lamb of God, you take away the sin of the world; have mercy on us. You are seated at the right hand of the Father; receive our prayer ..." and so on.

It saddens me, as no doubt it saddens some of you, that we gather to praise Cranmer's great work at a time when it has been battered and deformed in the unlikely cause of making it easier to understand. We seem to have forgotten that for solemn occasions we need exceptional and solemn language: something which transcends our everyday speech. We commend the "beauty of holiness", yet we forget the holiness of beauty. If we encourage the use of mean, trite, ordinary language we encourage a mean, trite and ordinary view of the world we inhabit.

If English is spoken in Heaven (as the spread of English as a world language makes more likely each year) God undoubtedly employs Cranmer as His speech-writer. The angels of the lesser ministries probably use the language of the New English Bible and the Alternative Service Book for internal memos.

The editors of the Revised Standard Version and the New English Bible had good reason for many of the changes they made to the King James Version. But a good many **more** changes were made just to lower the tone, in the belief that the rest of us wouldn't get the point if the word of God was a bit over our heads.

But the word of God is **supposed** to be a bit over our heads. Elevated is what God is. And for meddling with the Prayer Book there isn't even the scholarly excuse. The idea is to put great thoughts within our reach by changing the words. But the words **are** the thoughts. Admittedly the King James Version of the Bible asks us:

"Why take ye thought for raiment?"

But words aren't just decoration. They are the structure itself, as the Revised Standard Version inadvertently proves, by asking us:

"And why are you anxious about clothing?"

We can have a prayer book that talks like that if we want to -- a prayer book that talks like us on a bad day. But what will it say to us on a **really** bad day? Where is the comfort in a phrase too banal to be remembered? How can we be lifted up by a sentence which itself needs lifting on a stretcher?

"And if the salt have lost his savour," says the King James Version, "Wherewith shall it be salted?" Or as the Revised Standard Version so much less memorably puts it: "If salt has lost its taste how shall its saltiness be restored?"

Is it entirely an accident that the defacing of Cranmer's Prayer Book has coincided with a calamitous decline in literacy and the quality of English? We have rejected quality in expression, just as we have rejected quality in the buildings in which we work and educate. Fortunately many more people have begun to appreciate the extent of the problem we face and have seen the fundamental need for quality, for a respect for tradition, for humility before the ideas and practices of our forbears which served them so well, and for which we have yet to find anything like an effective replacement.

It is a remarkble fact that in these islands, we have produced the world's most successful language. That language has also served as the medium for some of the greatest literature in the world, including that of probably the greatest playwright who ever lived. Yet a great many people today look in dismay at what is happening to that language in the very place where it evolved. Looking at the way English is used in our popular newspapers, our radio and television programmes, or even in our schools and our theatres, they wonder what it is about our country and our society that our language has become so impoverished, so sloppy and so limited -- that we have arrived at such a dismal wasteland of banality, cliché and casual obscenity.

It leads me to wonder, for instance, how Hamlet would deliver his great "To be or not to be" soliloquy in the language of today -- "To be or not to be, that is the question, whether 'tis nobler in the mind ..." No, we can't have all that incomprehensible, high flown stuff. What about this?

> "Well, frankly, the problem as I see it at this moment in time is whether I should just lie down under all this hassle and let them walk all over me, or whether I should just say O.K., I get the message, and do myself in. I mean, let's face it, I'm in a no-win situation, and quite honestly I'm so stuffed up to here with the whole stupid mess that I can tell you I've just got a good mind to take the quick way out. That's the bottom line. The only problem is, what happens if I find that when I've bumped myself off there's some kind of a, you know, all that mystical stuff about when you die, you might find you're still -- know what I mean?"

In the last two decades we have witnessed a situation where our education has no longer been centred on the idea that the English language is an enormously precious legacy to be handed on with care. We have seen the abandonment of learning the rules of grammar and the parts of speech as boring and irrelevant. Learning poetry by heart has been abandoned, together with the idea of English as something really to be **learned**, by effort and application, by long and careful familiarity with those who had shown how to clothe their thought in the most precise, vivid and memorable language.

Of course there have been honourable exceptions to this rule where people have been courageous enough to withstand the accusations of being old-fashioned and reactionary. But the situation persists. At one of the country's leading public schools, for instance, I gather that George Eliot's *Middlemarch* was recently rejected from this year's list of 'A' Level English set books because it was thought to be too long and difficult.

Now, before I am accused of being unfair to teachers, let me hasten to add that I do not envy the task that teachers have, particularly in inner city schools. It must frequently appear a thankless task and I know that there are many who have been trying to uphold standards amidst the general spread of mediocrity. They need our sympathy and support in an exhausting task. English teachers inevitably have to teach their pupils what is relevant, but surely they should not teach **only** what is relevant. There is also a need, through great literature, to give their pupils -- in A.N. Whitehead's phrase -- "the habitual vision of greatness".

We do of course, have to recognize that we need ever higher standards if we are to survive in the modern competitive world. Our economic environment requires clarity in expression and precision in meaning. The world of work demands high standards of accuracy in communication skills to deploy and transmit facts, to process information, to persuade people, to sell goods. Many of you are familiar with computers and know that if you give these machines inaccurate instructions, your wishes will not be obeyed. So it is with people. If we do not communicate effectively with one another then we create confusion and lose our way.

Inevitably there has been controversy about the standards of English teaching in schools and about children's linguistic ability. This concern is not new. Complaints that young people cannot write grammatically, spell accurately, or express themselves clearly can be found stretching back into the last century. But there is now, I think, a growing consensus on what needs to be taught and it is heartening to witness the wide-spread recognition of this in the new national curriculum for English. It emphasises the importance of spelling, listening, reading and writing. It recognises the fact that competence in English is a key to success in all other subjects in the curriculum and a pre-requisite for adult life.

In the words of Saki -- "You can't expect a boy to be depraved until he has been to a good school!"

So today's prize is not merely an ode to antiquity. It is a demonstration of pride in our heritage. It recognises the contribution which that heritage makes to our daily life and to assuring the achievement of standards of quality that will serve our own children well in the future. Those standards are important because they help us to enlarge our awareness; to heighten and deepen our experience of life like nothing else can.

Dr. Johnson once remarked, "I know of no good prayers but those in *The Book of Common Prayer*." Ours is the age of miraculous writing machines but not of miraculous writing. Our banalities are no improvement on the past; merely an insult to it and a source of confusion in the present. In the case of our cherished religious writings, we should leave well alone, especially when it is better than well: when it is great. Otherwise we leave ourselves open to the terrible accusation once levelled by that true master of the banal, Samuel Goldwyn:

> "You've improved it worse."

I understand all the arguments about being contemporary and about the need to reflect the Spirit of the Age, but what alarms me is that the Age has no Spirit. It is all matter, and therefore, unable to endure.

SPEECH GIVEN BY H.R.H. THE PRINCE OF WALES AT THE AMERICAN INSTITUTE OF ARCHITECTS' 'ACCENT ON ARCHITECTURE' GALA DINNER

The National Building Museum, Washington, U.S.A.
22nd February, 1990

I MUST say, Ladies and Gentlemen, it is a mystery to me why you should want to invite me to one of your more prestigious evenings. I tried to make it as difficult for you as I could by saying I couldn't come on the evening before, which was the original date you had chosen. But no, you even changed the date. Is there an epidemic of masochism sweeping the ranks of the A.I.A.? While in Florida I read in the newspapers (it must be true....) that architects were queueing up to be "bashed" by the Prince -- apparently architect-bashing is my second favourite sport to polo. Somehow I don't think it would make a very good field sport because, unlike some others, the quarry has a nasty habit of shooting back!

Perhaps you have asked me because you lack excitement in your lives and, lurking deep down in every architect's subconscious, is a desire to live dangerously? The poor old R.I.B.A. (Royal Institute of British Architects) made a terrible error when they asked me to their 150th Anniversary dinner. The irony of it all is that I **assumed** they wanted me to make an after-dinner speech (like this evening), but that was not the case. Transatlantic fraternization seems to have led to a recent editorial in one of your magazines warning you not to become my 'pawns' -- in the way your English counterparts have become. I hadn't noticed that this was the case, I must say, but perhaps, on this occasion, I can add a little 'sauce piquante' to the 'pawn cocktail' gathered here.

I hope you realize how difficult it is to address such a distinguished assembly outside Great Britain. Choosing a theme has nearly ruined my health.... Apart from anything else, I don't want to create a diplomatic incident -- particularly as I read somewhere recently that President Bush is supposed to be a 13th cousin of my wife! I am also conscious that I may easily be accused of Royal interference in American domestic affairs.

There has been an exchange of architectural talent between our two countries for a long time, albeit until recently on a fairly modest scale. There are one or two buildings in London which stand out by their quality and which, upon further examination, turn out to have been designed or inspired by Americans. The first store in London to rival your department stores -- Selfridges on Oxford Street -- has really never been bettered as a civilized piece of 'retail development'. Bush House -- famed as the home of the BBC World Service -- was designed by an American. The sculpture gallery at the Tate, which has just been restored to its full classical grandeur, is by the same John Russell Pope who is responsible for your National Gallery here in Washington.

'Exchange' has also occurred in the opposite direction -- despite Thomas Jefferson's unpromising comment that "English architecture is in the most wretched style I ever saw". I think he might have revised this opinion had he seen the Residence at the British Embassy here in Washington, designed by the incomparable Sir Edwin Lutyens. And the designer of the original Capitol -- the Frenchman Benjamin Latrobe -- learnt his art under England's Sir John Soane. This cultural exchange continues between us today, and is increasing -- in quantity if not always in quality! There is much of positive value that our two cultures share. However our cities also share a number of unfortunate legacies from the past, and vision is going to be needed among architects and developers if we are to be able to cope with these.

I'm sure many of you were sorry to hear recently of the death of the planner/ philosopher Lewis Mumford, who drew a great deal of his inspiration from the other side of the Atlantic. I am sure that everyone here would hope that, even though he is no longer with us, Mumford's writings will continue to stimulate those who encounter them. No one, I am certain, would seriously advocate that we take this opportunity to clear the shelves of the libraries of the world of Mumford's books. Yet, unbelievably, this century began with such a plea from the world of architects and builders. One architect who made this plea was the Italian futurist Antonio Sant 'Elia, whose undeniably impressive drawings have just been on show in London. Sant 'Elia was so intoxicated by the pace of change and the glamour of the machine that he looked forward to the day when buildings would last less time than we do, and each generation would have to build its own cities -- the epitome of the throw-away society. If that comes about, and we seem to be heading in that direction, then I shall be proud to be considered old-fashioned, reactionary, antediluvian, anachronistic -- you name it!

Why **should** every generation be required to wipe the slate clean? Can't we be allowed to hold on to things of value from the past? And might we not pass on to our children something of what **we** have learned? I wouldn't agree with Mumford on everything, but he succinctly summed up my own view of Sant 'Elia's mentality, and that of his followers, when he said: "If you fall in love with a machine there is something wrong with your love life. If you worship a machine there is something wrong with your religion." May I add to this that I feel that if you find yourself having to **live or work** in a building that derives its inspiration from a purely mechanical or technological source, there is something wrong with your architect? What, after all, is architecture for? Or rather, **who** is it for? The answer now -- as we approach the twenty-first century -- it seems to me, is the same as it has always been. It is for human beings.

I understand all the arguments about being contemporary and about the need to reflect the Spirit of the Age, but what alarms me is that the Age has no Spirit. It is all matter, and therefore unable to endure. Our built environment seems to reflect the underlying misconception that we are the only generation on this earth and that we are here to do with it as we please. We could perhaps learn from the Hopi Indians of North America whose every action was dependent on the effect it would have on the seventh unborn generation. The problem we have, it seems to me, is over the metaphor of time. Linear time justifies this modern obsession with change, for its own sake, and is based on Nihilism in the sense that the line stretches to an unknown future in one direction and an unknowable past in the other. Plato and the sages predominantly talk of time as a circle -- or series of circles -- so that the illusion of 'passing time' is the movement around the periphery of the circle. Wisdom, surely, invites us towards the heart of time which is the non-moving centre of the circle. Perhaps the mounting environmental crisis the world faces will concentrate our minds and restore a degree of sanity to our outlook? Perhaps then we will begin to rediscover that human values, the things of the spirit which **are** surely, divinely or mysteriously inspired, are the only ones which endure. They don't need to be re-invented each generation, but they **do** need to be passed on and nurtured from generation to generation.

Architecture, as Jefferson realized, is the pre-eminent embodiment of a nation's values. It never lies about where our priorities are. Ours may be an age of vast wealth, but what can we **see** of it? It sometimes seems to me that the richer we get, the **uglier** we tend to make our surroundings. What is worse, not only do we seem to have mislaid the ability to **create** beauty, but we also set out to destroy what beauty there is left in the world. The nineteenth-century English writer John Ruskin, whose books on architecture were also highly influential on **these** shores, would have called this an age not of wealth, but of "**illth**" -- a term he used to describe money which was poured into the production of objects, and the creation of places, which diminished rather than enriched the life of man. There was, for Ruskin, "no wealth but life". He **would** have approved, I am sure, of your choice of Gold Medallist this year. Indeed Fay Jones' master, Frank Lloyd Wright, derived profound inspiration from Ruskin. Architecture began as a craft, then it became a conscious art -- now it seems to be **just** a science. Surely we need to **regain** the art and the craft, and then combine them with the science. This is just what Fay Jones is doing in his way -- and by so doing he has put our feet back on the ground.

So there is **another** tradition at work here, among architects such as Fay Jones, which is just as vital and just as 'American' as the classical tradition. Fay Jones' buildings speak of what Ruskin termed "The Poetry of Architecture" -- a poetry arising out of buildings in harmony with their natural surroundings. They seem to evoke the amplitude of Nature -- without damaging Nature. His Thorncroft Chapel was built in the woods from timber carried to the site by hand. Not one of the trees around it was touched. "Good architecture," Fay Jones said, "has the potential to nourish." The creative process, for him, "attempts to transcend utility and technology and express something of greater human meaning".

Maybe, gradually, we are about to witness the beginnings of another age of architecture. Maybe like an elephant, it requires a long gestation period, but as in the pachydermal case its longevity may be substantial. The time has surely now arrived when we **must** learn to work **with** rather than **against** Nature; when we can once again make places in which to live and work which are more than 'machines', rather places in which we can not only **have our being**, but enrich our perceptions of what our being really is. It is in Nature that we discover the source of many of our human values.

The really interesting challenge, I believe, lies in whether we can apply the 'timeless' lessons of the past, and a love of natural forms, to the development of office buildings, in a city like New York or London in the 21st century. Why can't we create a cityscape or townscape which engenders a sense of pride and belonging, and which raises our spirits? Why on earth, is it considered 'immoral' in architectural circles if the outside of a building does not reflect the function of the inside? Can't we bring our rediscovered sense of Nature's value, and our human scale, to bear upon the design of wholly **new** towns and cities? It has been said to me that property developers are the "Medici of the twentieth century". Where then is our Florence? And why is a great city like London seen by our "Medici" as merely a financial staging post between New York and Tokyo? Where has that spirit of patronage gone which always sought to offer the rarest and most magnificent examples of the architect's gratitude for a city of which one could be proud? The architecture of a country is determined ultimately by the people who **pay** for it, but it should be sure to celebrate more than just **economic** values.

There does seem precious little room in our **present** way of doing things for the timeless values to reappear. We might begin by paying more attention to those **for** whom we build. I am **not** arguing for a return to the Age of Faith which gave us our great Cathedrals, but I would hope we might strive for an Age of Reverence -- reverence for what gives us life, and for the fragile world in which we live.

In this regard it is perhaps instructive to listen for a moment to the resonant wisdom of Chief Seattle who, in 1854 wrote a letter in response to the U.S. Government's proposal to purchase his tribe's territory in exchange for a regulated life on a reservation. This is what he said:

> Man did not weave the web of life; he is merely a strand in it. Whatever he does to the web he does to himself.
>
> How can you buy or sell the sky, the warmth of the land? The idea is strange to us. Every part of this earth is sacred to my people. Every shining pine needle, every sandy shore. Every mist in the dark woods, every clearing and humming insect is holy in the memory and experience of my people. We are part of the Earth and it is part of us. We know that the white man does not understand our ways. One portion of the land is the

> same to him as the next, for he is a stranger who comes in the night and takes from it whatever he needs. The Earth is not his brother, but his enemy, and when he has conquered it he moves on.

In our own day it seems that many patrons of commercial buildings are intent on putting their 'signatures' on the skyline. Much of the commercial building of today bears as much relation to architecture as advertising slogans bear to literature. The architects of 'Signature Buildings' ransack History as if it were a wardrobe full of old clothes. Their buildings seldom bear any meaningful relationship to the areas in which they are placed.

I hope that when this latest fashion is played out a way of building will emerge which recognizes the **whole** picture of human life in our cities. I'm sure that our increasing environmental consciousness will lead us to that. Developers are certainly now having to take the environmental impact of what they do very seriously. One thing which growing environmental awareness is doing is that it is **forcing** governments and businessmen to think again about the way costs and profits are calculated. For example, the hitherto ignored or hidden costs of pollution and energy waste will have to be taken into account in the future. Can property developers not go one step further and begin to think more of the **human** and natural costs of development and begin to see this as economic good sense and not just idealism? We are gradually coming to realize that the long-term calculation is better **business** than the short-term.

One very important example of the challenge that I would like to see faced, and which might interest you, is the development of Paternoster Square in London, next to St. Paul's Cathedral. St. Paul's Dome is not just a bowler hat perched on top of a business-suited City. It has deep significance for both our nations -- containing as it does an Anglo-American shrine to the dead of the Second World War -- and is very much the heart of our own capital city. (It's also a good place to get married!) Because of this fact I believe that very great care should be taken over this site. There is a huge challenge here for the Anglo-American combination of Park Tower of New York and Greycoat of London, this project is far more than just the enterprise of two developers. I am pleased to note another example of that architectural 'exchange' between our two nations, now that Park Tower of New York and Greycoat, who have teamed up in the development of the square. However, this project is far more than just the enterprise of two developers. It should be seen as the joint effort of the people of our two nations to ensure that something of real, enduring value is created next to that great building whose architect -- Wren -- you are now celebrating with an exhibition in Washington which I saw this afternoon.

We will be assisted in this, I'm sure, by the good sense and vigilance of the planners in the City of London -- who are not to be won over by a few Corinthian columns. And in addition, I hope that the developer will see the need for some kind of voluntary urban framework -- what has been called a **code** -- which can ensure that whatever buildings are erected on the site, they will not compete for attention with each other or with St. Paul's, but will create a human-scaled, coherent and living piece of City. Think of those great towns and cities with their memorable cathedral precincts. You all know them. What makes them so special? I would suggest it is the sense of pride and belonging they engender; the civilized values they represent; the design of enclosed space inspired by what is 'in the public good', as much as in the commercial interest of the business world. They raise our spirits in a way that is hard to define. Developers, architects, journalists, critics, planners want to live in such areas. People like me have parents who need to use such places for great ceremonies of state. And the buildings pay humble homage to the noble structure in their midst. So why can't we try to reorganize **our** values a little and build with this aim in mind? Why, if so many intelligent people spend their holidays in beautiful towns and cities, or in exquisite hill villages in Italy or France, do they persist in dismissing any attempt to do so as an obsession with an irrelevant past -- as pastiche; as Disneyland? "What does it profit a man if he gains the world, but loses his own soul?"

Naturally, the developers of this important site have every right to expect a reasonable profit, and a development which is attractive to investors. What I question is whether there is only one way of achieving these ends. I believe that if Paternoster Square is to be both a vindication of tradition, and a model for the next century, a number of twentieth-century developers' instincts will have to be suspended to make room for real thought: the instinct to create as much undifferentiated floor area as possible -- in the interests of 'flexibility'; the instinct to build quickly, cheaply and thinly; the instinct to go up as high as regulations will allow: and the instinct to develop unrestrained by the recognition of human needs. We cannot and should not ignore the possibilities that technology offers us. But we must be masters of our technology, and not its tools. The 'balance' we now seek between ourselves and Nature we must also seek in our approach to our cities.

Since the Age of the Enlightenment, Man has tended to assume God-like powers over Nature and his surroundings, seeking to dominate them. But we don't **have** to keep on rushing headlong into the 'future' as if the whole of history were a hundred yard dash. As Mahatma Ghandi said: "There is more to life than going faster." We **can** permit ourselves to move 'inward' -- into tradition -- and 'outward' -- into Nature -- and 'upward' -- to the heavens, along the way. Poets have always been more aware of this than economists. T.S. Eliot seems to me to be speaking of a different conception of time when he writes:

> We shall not cease from exploration
> And the end of all our exploration
> Will be to arrive where we started
> And know the place for the first time.

And it is open to us to rediscover this conception of time. Professor Christopher Alexander writes of a '**Timeless** Way' of building through which "the order of a building or a town grows directly from the inner nature of the people ... who are in it."

Our cities don't need to grow uncontrollably. We must surely accept some framework of restraint which might restore a healthy balance to our urban environment, and restore the equilibrium between buildings and Nature. These matters lead us to some of the central questions of our times. What does it mean to be **truly** human and what is a fitting way to house this human-ness? How much influence does the design of the built environment actually have on the well-being of human beings; on their sense of belonging and hence on the relationship an individual has with his fellow man --in other words, the community? And what, in the end, should be our relationship with Nature? These are **large** questions, but it has been said that civilizations are built on the questions they raise. Maybe these questions are a proper foundation upon which we can build. This may be an ambitious hope, but one which I'm sure will not be beyond a distinguished company such as yourselves.

It is, surely, a privilege to have the gifts of design and creativity and to be able to put them at the service of mankind. Believe me when I say that I appreciate how difficult the role of an architect is. As the progenitors of the built environment the only public art form that affects **all** of us, you carry so many of our subconscious expectations on your shoulders. Somewhere along the line the education of architects (and developers!) has abandoned this sensitivity to the basic feelings of the ordinary citizen. But that is another story -- and contained in a speech yet to come....!

If we look back through history, the roll call of talented British linguists is remarkable. Queen Elizabeth I, for example, spoke no fewer than seven languages. Many of the classic and still unsurpassed translations from the literature of the Arab, Persian, Chinese and Japanese civilizations, made in the 19th and early 20th centuries by such luminaries as Sir Richard Burton, Edward Fitzgerald and Arthur Waley, have stood the test of time.

ADDRESS BY H.R.H. THE PRINCE OF WALES TO THE ROYAL SOCIETY FOR THE ARTS

23rd May, 1990

FOREIGN LANGUAGES FOR THE NEW EUROPE

Mr. Chairman, Ladies and Gentlemen,

WHY IS IT that, when standing here, I am assailed by an extraordinary feeling of 'déjà vu'? Many of the faces in the audience look familiar. Have I come on the right day? Perhaps you are expecting me to address you on a different subject from the one I thought I had prepared? Perhaps it is all a dream and when I wake up I will find that everyone else has been asleep....

We are meeting at a time of dramatic international change. Relations between East and West are improving; the countries of Eastern Europe have, one by one, as we saw in Hungary recently, cast off the dead hand of a communism imposed on them from outside, reasserting their desire to run their own affairs as they see best; further afield, co-operation between the countries of the Pacific Rim and the West continues to develop at great speed, particularly in the commercial and economic spheres. All this at a time when the members of the European Community are redoubling their efforts to achieve an economic and, perhaps, a political union of a new kind. These developments present enormous new challenges to the United Kingdom, and enormous opportunities. In my remarks today, I intend to concentrate on one of those challenges: the need for Britain urgently to make up lost ground in the learning of foreign languages.

Over the centuries, a number of languages have served as the *lingui franca* of the civilized world -- Greek, Latin, French and, in the second half of the 20th century, English. Believe it or not, in 1689 the Treaty of Nerchinsk between Russia and China was negotiated in Latin by a Pole, a Frenchman and a Portuguese. Remember, too, Sir Charles Napier's economical use of the Latin language when he reported the capture of Sind with his famous one-word despatch "Peccavi".[1]

There are a number of advantages in having as one's native tongue the world's principle international language -- business benefits, our cultural exports benefit, the British point of view can be easily understood. But there are also dangers. One -- as I pointed out in my speech at the presentation of the Thomas Cranmer Schools Prize last December -- is that the quality of our language can all too easily be reduced to the lowest common denominator of non-native English speakers. At a recent Anglo-Japanese conference, a spokesman from Japan asserted that the world's most widely-spoken language today was "broken English". The other major danger is that we lull ourselves into an arrogant but false sense of security, believing that, as the rest of the world learns English, there is no need for us to learn their languages.

Anyone tempted to believe this fallacy should reflect on the world-wide reputation of the BBC. Its English language radio broadcasts are indeed of the highest standard. But one of the reasons for the respect in which it is held is that a window on the world -- and on the United Kingdom -- is offered to countless millions of listeners through no fewer than 37 different vernacular services.

Within two years, Britain will find itself part of a single market and, in effect, a single population of three hundred and twenty million people, 82% of whom do not have English as their mother tongue. As the European Community's relations with Central and Eastern Europe develop -- as they are bound to -- native English speakers will find themselves in an even smaller minority. To all of those people however, British firms will wish to sell their goods; with all of them British people will wish -- and need -- to communicate.

---

1. Peccavi (Latin) means 'I have sinned'.

Business no longer recognizes national frontiers. Just look at the cross-border take overs and mergers which are announced almost every day: $40 billion worth within the EC alone in 1989. What serious international company is going to select its future leaders from people who are not as much at ease in Paris, Frankfurt, Rome or, indeed, Tokyo as they are in London or Glasgow? And yet, how often do we see British commercial representatives at trade fairs abroad hard put to communicate with their potential customers because they speak no language other than English?

At this point I must confess that I may not be the ideal pot to call other kettles black! My French is marginally passable -- I obtained a reasonable 'A' level -- but I lack the kind of linguistic, colloquial confidence which comes from imbibing the language and culture at source. I am the kind of Englishman who finds conversing in a foreign language is made much easier with the assistance of a small alcoholic beverage! Maybe that is why I succeeded in failing my 'O' level German -- alcohol was restricted at school! Making the **effort** to speak someone else's language is what counts. People appreciate it. It makes a good impression, which is so vital in business.

I am reminded of the angry reply sent by a French businessman who, after repeated attempts to get through to his trading partner in Britain on the telephone, sent the following exasperated telex: "Lorsque nou téléphonons, votre standardiste ne connaît pas le français et raccroche le téléphone tout simplement sans chercher. Vous voudrez bien luiexpliquer que l'anglais est certes une langue merveilleuse mais pas encore universelle. Si vou voulez continuer à travailler avec l'étranger il vous faudra faire un effort. C'est ce que font toutes les autre nations."[1] I wonder how far our **current** trade deficit is attributable to the low priority which British business has given to language training in the past?

It is tempting to argue in favour of cost-effective 'quick fixes', such as hiring translators or, for particular jobs, linguistic experts. This attitude is dangerously misleading. Languages are inseparable from their culture. A translating machine has no understanding of the history, values, and culture of society.

---

1. When we telephone, your operator doesn't know French and quite simply hangs up without further ado. It would be advisable to explain to her that English, while being a marvellous language is not yet universal. If you want to go on working with other countries you will have to make an effort. That's what all other countries are doing.

Setting up business in a new country, without adequate knowledge of its culture, can lead to costly mistakes, and endless misunderstandings. Second-hand knowledge is all too often second-class knowledge.

One of our most distinguished politicians told me years ago of a speech he once delivered during a visit to the Soviet Union. He thought it would make a good impression to say his opening words in Russian, and duly did so, having noted down as he drove through Moscow what he thought was 'Ladies and Gentlemen' in Russian. Why, he asked his staff later, was there a stunned silence and no applause? "They would have appreciated it better, Sir," came the reply, "if you hadn't referred to 'Ladies and Gentlemen' as 'urinals and water closets'!"

My namesake Charles V, Emperor of the Holy Roman Empire, took the view that one could judge a man by the number of languages he spoke: "un hombre vale tantos come idiomas sabe." It is easy to forget, too, that learning foreign languages provides heightened awareness of one's own culture and civilization. Goethe, that great German poet, put it very concisely: "Wer fremde Sprachen nicht kennt, weiss nichts von seiner eigenen" : "Those who know no foreign languages know nothing of their own."

Encouragingly, there is growing evidence of the cross-curricular value of learning languages at school. The Modern Language Working Group's initial report on the National Curriculum, published in March, makes the point that "because the study of modern languages involves relearning how to express oneself, it is well suited to dealing with subjects as varied as history, geography, design and technology, maths and sciences".

Clear as the case is for learning languages, our failings in this area go back a long way. Attention has been drawn to it in a variety of reports over the years -- the 1947 Scarborough Commission, the 1961 Hayter Enquiry for the University Grants Committee, Sir Peter Parker's 1986 enquiry "Speaking for the Future" and, just this month, by the House of Lords Select Committee on the European Communities. In fits and spasms, we have reminded ourselves of the need to do better. Far too rarely have we followed up with specific programmes. Today, with the approach of 1992, and such stimulations as the Department of Trade and Industry's current campaign to encourage businessmen to learn foreign languages, I believe that the message is at last getting across: our opinion-formers understand that Britain's prosperity and influence in the future will depend very largely on our knowledge and mastery of the languages spoken by our partners.

It is none too soon. In 1978, our hosts today, The Royal Society of Arts, carried out a survey of some 200 exporting firms which showed a distinct correlation between export success and the employment of export executives proficient in foreign languages. Ten years later, in 1988, Stephen Hagen of Newcastle Polytechnic, in a survey which produced responses from more than eleven hundred British companies, revealed that some 44% of British business believed that it could significantly improve its trade performance if it had better access to foreign language expertise.

It is instructive to see what our partners have been doing. Major European industrial groups such as Thomson, Hoechst, Bayer, Siemens, all have well-developed in-house language training centres. Siemens, for example, spend almost £1.5 million each year -- around half of their total training budget -- on foreign language training -- 40% of it on languages other than English. In France, the network of Chambers of Commerce operates150 'Centres d'étude des langues' across the country. Ten thousand firms use the service each year, training some 60,000 employees in 22 different languages.

How many British firms, I wonder, have carried out any serious analysis of their language needs and resources, and evolved an appropriate strategy? Our business schools enjoy a high reputation. But how many include the learning of a foreign language as a compulsory part of their programme? The Fontainebleau School of Management in France, on the other hand, requires proven competence in at least three languages as a **condition** of entry!

In brief: the competition knows what it is doing. I see a real danger that by putting itself at a competitive disadvantage in linguistic skills, British business will lose out more generally and find itself left on the touchline as others challenge for Europe's industrial supremacy. And Britain will find itself increasingly under-represented in those international organizations and institutions which play an ever-increasing role in all our lives.

There **are** success stories, of course. The British Tourist Authority, for example, launched a campaign three months ago to improve foreign language skills in our tourism companies, following the publication of a damning report entitled -- very appropriately -- *Lost for Words*, which revealed the complete absence of a language training programme for staff employed to look after foreign visitors to this country.

Small firms, whose survival depends on exporting increasingly, understand the need for their staff to speak foreign languages. Big ones too are, in places, getting the message: one of our largest manufacturers of car batteries recently won a £2 million order from North Africa, very largely because the telephonist spoke French. But we still have a long way to go.

There is a popular myth that the British are no good at languages. In my own case, as I said earlier, this is all too true. My sister and I were lucky enough to have two French tutors at different periods during the summer holidays when we were small -- but we spent all our time trying to escape from them! With so much continental blood coursing through my veins, I should have done better. While I was in the Royal Navy, I asked to do a Naval interpreter's course in French, but for some reason my request was turned down.

This was a pity because I might otherwise have performed more creditably when President Mitterrand asked me at a European Community Lunch at Buckingham Palace to interpret for him as he wanted to tell Herr Helmut Schmidt, the then Federal Chancellor, a story. Picture the situation -- The French President couldn't speak German, the German Chancellor couldn't speak French. I hadn't done French dictation since I was at school! The result was disastrous. Monsieur Mitterrand lost me in the first line of the first sentence when he began, "Un vieux savant ..." Panic descended on my overloaded brain. "An old soap ..." I translated to myself.... It **can't** be possible. Two sentences later, the President gave up in disgust and went off to find a more competent interpreter!

However, if we look back through history, the roll call of talented British linguists is remarkable. Queen Elizabeth I, for example, spoke no fewer than seven languages. Many of the classic and still unsurpassed translations from the literature of the Arab, Persian, Chinese and Japanese civilizations made in the 19th and early 20th centuries by such luminaries as Sir Richard Burton, Edward Fitzgerald and Arthur Waley, have stood the test of time. Even today, there is good evidence that, when properly taught and well motivated, British linguists are as good as any in the world. So we cannot shelter behind the excuse of national ineptitude.

The rot, I fear, set in with the decline of The British Empire and the loss of a sense of purpose and even of mission. As Britain's former colonies and dominions acquired independence, and our transatlantic links took on new significance, American English established itself more and more as the ubiquitous common language of the Anglo-Saxon world -- and beyond.

In 1953, the General Certificate of Education compounded the rot by dropping its compulsory foreign language requirement, and reduced the number of subjects studied at 'A' level. Gone was German for scientists, French for economists. In came specialization at the expense of broader education.

At university level and in the business sector, the post-war period also saw a decline of interest in language study programmes, particularly in the areas of Asian and African studies of which the commercial and political importance is now increasing.

Here, as in other areas, it seems to me that business has suffered from an ingrained short-term outlook rooted in the insatiable appetite of the Stock Market for ever better bottom lines. Our competitors are often far more well-equipped to plan for the future as a result, for example, of the longer-term thinking adopted by the banks and institutions which -- to a greater extent than is the case in Britain --control the Boards of leading industrial corporations. Governments, too, have played their part in our competitors' successes: in both France and Germany there are generous tax concessions for business-led language training programmes. Need I say more...?

If we are to make a serious impact upon our national deficiencies in this field, then action will have to be taken in three areas: in schools, in our universities, and in the business sector.

First, the schools. It is said that foreign languages are the most hated subjects in our schools today. And the figures show that the number of pupils taking foreign languages at 'A' level has fallen sharply over the last decade. (We are in any case **way** behind all our major competitors in the proportion of our pupils who stay on at school after the age of 16 -- but **that** is another problem!)

Almost forty years after the GCE (General Certificate of Education) dropped the foreign language requirement, the National Curriculum is, at last, reinstating it. All secondary school-children up to the age of 16 will have to take at least **one** foreign language. This is a major step in the right direction -- even if it does little to extend the learning of languages at an advanced level. We must also recognize the danger that the demands of the National Curriculum and the overwhelming present emphasis on French could, paradoxically, squeeze out the scope for learning second or even third foreign languages.

All too often, it seems to me, learning languages has been seen as a thankless routine of learning by heart remote texts and long lists of words which have nothing to do with asking your way on the Paris Metro. Do you remember the scholastic horror of having to get up in front of your class and speak French out aloud? There was always some frightful little brute in the back row at the *moment critique* to destroy your linguistic pretensions.

Over the last fifteen years, however, there have been radical improvements in language teaching techniques.

Satellite television, video and computers have all played their role. Schools now use authentic materials, organize role plays, simulations, group and project work, and increasingly organize visits and exchanges with foreign countries. Some of our schools are developing their international links even more widely, offering as an option the International Baccalureat in place of 'A' levels. I see all this as enormously encouraging: not only does it clearly give language studies the emphasis they deserve, but it also points the way towards ever-closer international co-operation in educational standards.

But every teaching scheme, however well conceived, depends for its success on the availability of good and committed teachers. It is now clear that, even to implement the single compulsory language requirement of the new National Curriculum, we need to find thousands more language teachers. Perhaps we could entice some of our retired teachers back to work? But what I would very much hope is that the most **serious** consideration will also be given to filling the gap with native foreign-language speakers brought in from other countries.

This is how our counterparts meet their English language training requirements -- with the active support of the British Council. Over the past twelve years the Japanese government has recruited more than 1,000 British nationals to teach English in Japan. For years, French, German and Spanish have been taught in British schools with the help of 'Assistants'. But they were always regarded as an optional extra, rather than the core of the teaching process. We should, in my view, make much better use of foreign teachers, not least of their ability to make foreign language-learning fun and to introduce that vital ingredient of cultural education.

There is one other area which, it seems to me, provides an important, hitherto untapped source of expertise. We have in the United Kingdom many ethnic minorities with their own strong cultural and linguistic identities. Naturally -- and rightly -- they are keen to preserve these. This concept of dual identity is as important for those on the Celtic fringes of the United Kingdom as it is for those who come from further afield.

It seems such a waste for the rest of us not to take advantage of their knowledge of languages other than English, and to learn from them. Before being invested as Prince of Wales in 1969, I felt it was important to make at least **some** effort to learn the Welsh language. Lloyd George -- whose Welsh was rather better than mine -- always claimed that his ability to consult his advisers in his native language during the Versailles conference in 1919 gave his negotiations an extra edge!

I do hope that the changes implemented in the National Curriculum will lead to more and more pupils taking foreign languages in the Sixth Form, and subsequently at College and University. This is the second area where we need to catch up. It seems to me vital that the universities should plan now for a major expansion of foreign language teaching -- not just of the familiar European languages, but also of the Oriental and African languages the decline of which was the main subject of Sir Peter Parker's 1986 report. And our colleges need to develop further today's welcome trend towards degree courses combining languages with other skills.

Whatever efforts may be made in our schools and universities to remedy current shortcomings, the impact on our national performance will be minimal unless industry and business demonstrate that they, too, attach major importance to the acquisition of foreign language skills. The commitment must be clear at the recruitment stage so that young people can see for themselves that it is worth making the effort to master foreign languages. It must also be clear at the corporate level. We must grasp the simple truth that knowledge of foreign languages is not an end in itself, but an essential skill for anyone seeking to make their mark, in whatever discipline, including science, technology and even law, at international level.

At this point I have a feeling that several of you may be shifting uneasily in your seats. You may be thinking that I am totally out of touch with the realities of the business world and what I have been talking about is yet another luxury which business cannot afford -- like environmental considerations or corporate involvement in the community. Of course, there are always reasons for postponing awkward decisions involving spending money; all I am trying to say is that, if we go on shelving the issue, we shall put ourselves at a severe disadvantage and become an increasingly insignificant trading nation on the periphery of everyone else.

One of the key recommendations of the House of Lords Report on European Schools and Language Learning in the United Kingdom reads: "The attitude of British society towards modern foreign language training must change. All sectors of society must be convinced of the relevance of foreign language learning as a communication tool." I could not agree more. But I doubt if anyone will pay much attention to those recommendations.

In certain areas, as I have tried to show, the message is beginning to get across. It is vital, however, that the momentum is sustained, until it becomes as much second nature to all of us as it is to our counterparts in other countries to speak foreign languages. Independent studies have found that the impetus and priority imparted to foreign language studies by the reports of Lord Scarborough and Lord Hayter steadily diminished over the following years, to the extent that it became impossible to discern **any** active national policy in the field of language studies. Why is it, do you think, that as a nation we consistently fail to see the point of investing money **now** in order to reap the reward **later**? I would submit that we could pick up a few hints from our continental colleagues in this regard, but that would be expecting a lot....

Four years ago, Sir Peter Parker called for the establishment of a permanent monitoring system which would allow us to tell, at a glance, the level of our national expertise in foreign languages, in the hope that -- to take but one example -- we would not unwittingly find ourselves in such a crisis as that posed by the acute shortage of foreign language teachers today.

I continue to believe that this is a proposal worth following up -- however belatedly. But we need to do it **now** since we are already a long way behind.

How familiar that all sounds. I remember making a speech in 1987 to the Royal Society for Asian Affairs in which I commended Sir Peter Parker's efforts -- but very little has changed since then. To delay further is, surely, folly. How, precisely, we should follow up this proposal needs further thought.

But we could do much worse than establish a partnership of all those with a stake in the success of our language learning programmes -- in which I should be glad to play whatever part was considered helpful -- to carry out regular reviews of what has been achieved, and what remains to be done.

With the advent of the single European market, the rapid progress towards a unified Germany and the other changes to the world's political landscape taking place almost daily, we cannot afford further mistakes. There is nothing charitable or philanthropic in what I am suggesting, merely hard-nosed self-interest. I can assure you that I am not standing up here making a fool of myself because, like a fibre diet, it might be good for my health. Nor am I doing so because I find a perverse satisfaction in criticizing people or, as some have deduced, because I hail from the ranks of the frustrated unemployed. No -- I am trying to provoke a reaction because I believe what I have been saying is in our overall national interest.

Perhaps Goethe was right -- once again -- when he wrote one hundred and eighty years ago --

> "Wer die deutsche Sprache versteht und studiert, befindet sich auf dem Markte, wo alle Nationen ihre Waren anbieten; er spielt den Dolmetscher, indem er sich selbst bereichert."

For the benefit of those whose German is as bad as mine, I offer the following free translation: "Those who understand and study German are right in the market place where all the nations are busy offering their goods, so that they can act as interpreters and make themselves wealthy into the bargain." As Alphonse Karr put it a mere 140 years ago, "Plus ça change, plus c'est la même chose".[1]

---

1. French -- "More change, more of the same."

I do hope the assembled group will concentrate on the themes I have touched upon. A sense of partnership and dialogue that respects sovereign rights, a recognition that poverty is a key factor in environmental destruction, and that the solution to this involves liberating the human spirit and entrepreneurial effort from unnecessary bureaucracy, unacceptable corruption and inequity everywhere.

SPEECH GIVEN BY H.R.H. THE PRINCE OF WALES TO OBSERVER-INTERNATIONAL INSTITUTE FOR ENVIRONMENT & DEVELOPMENT CONFERENCE

19th March, 1991

Mr. Trelford, Ladies and Gentlemen,

IF I MAY say so, I am enormously flattered to be included in this list of highly eminent speakers today, and am suitably humble. I must also admit at this point that I usually get into terrible trouble whenever I address a conference in this particular hall, so I dread to think what might happen today.

Richard Sandbrook knows all about getting into trouble. Any of you who may not be aware of this should have read an article in the *Daily Telegraph* last week about what he used to get up to as a student. He and I were at university at about the same time. We seem to be about the same age; he's a year older than I am. I was down the road at Cambridge University and he was at East Anglia. In those days I believe he was rather a rebellious student leader in the late '60's. Now he's becoming ever more establishment-orientated I would suggest. I was extremely quiet, on the contrary, in my student days, but now I'm becoming ever more rebellious. It's finally proved to me conclusively what I always feared, and that is that I'm a very late developer, which is why I'm here at this conference on development.

Now, Ladies and Gentlemen, there may still be people who are under the illusion that the world we face in the future will be more comfortable than the one we have now; that we can go on as we are, confidently predicting that 'progress' will continue indefinitely, and that technology will find the answers to all our problems. They may be right, and people like me who point to alarming signs of environmental and social stress may just be alarmist and pessimistic cranks, but I suggest the evidence needs careful examination.

Right now, up to 15 million people are at risk in the drylands of Africa. They suffer from an apparently unbreakable cycle of environmental degradation and drought leading to poverty and hunger and yet more environmental stress. Tragic and disgraceful though it is, death seems to be the only obvious way out at present for these unfortunate people.

Elsewhere, millions more are already suffering from the pollution and shortage of water. Last year's Children's summit revealed that nine million children die prematurely from water-borne disease every year. In urban areas of the Third World, millions of people have no secure shelter, and little or no protection from atmospheric and water-borne pollution. In rural areas, whole ecosystems are under threat from the hunger for land for growing food and the search for fuel. In the forests, in the range lands and in the upland areas, people struggle to live directly from what is left of Nature's wealth. Four-fifths of the human family still rely on wood as their primary fuel. Population pressures and unsustainable agriculture lead to soil erosion which threatens future livelihoods as well as biological diversity.

The possibility (some would say the probability) of serious climate change makes future prospects worse, and with over five hundred oil wells still burning in Kuwait we don't need any other reminder of the speed with which technological wizardry can be turned into environmental devastation. Altogether it is a sad and depressing scenario.

Now, although it may sound gloomy to say so, it is my belief that until more people concentrate on development which meets basic human needs, combined with enlightened stewardship of Nature's capital, human and environmental tragedies will continue to unfold. All the evidence suggests that population numbers will continue to rise from 5.4 billion now to 8.4 billion by 2025. One result will be an ever-growing proportion of young people. Already, for example, (and I'm sure Professor Goldemberg will correct me if I'm wrong) 50% of Brazil's population is under 25. By the year 2000 it is estimated that in Africa 44% of the population will be under the age of 14, compared with just

20% here, but I don't need to tell all of you that. All the signs are that many of them will live in urban and rural poverty with no prospects of a secure livelihood. That is unless human tragedy on a massive scale comes first. But surely it is crazy to wait for ecological and human catastrophes before we tackle the root causes of them, even though the lessons of history are not always very encouraging in this particular regard. We can act **now** to change the outlook.

I believe there is really no alternative to striving for sustainable development. There are two reasons for this conclusion. First and foremost is the moral or humanitarian imperative. Second is the global insecurity that poverty and environmental destruction will create for all of us. It was the President of that sensible and far-sighted organization, The International Institute for Environment and Development, Sir Crispin Tickell, who observed that we can expect to see a rapid rise in the number of environmental refugees, driven from their homes by mounting environmental stress occasioned by possible climate changes, continued over-use of natural resources and exacerbated by disputes over what remains of scarce resources, such as water. In other words, the frightening scenario of millions of people on the move, literally in search of survival, leading to entirely new threats to global security.

Naturally the problems are always someone else's fault. People point to the greed of the North, the corruption of the South, the short-term outlook of industry, the equally short-term outlook of politicians and the overstatements of environmentalists -- even, perhaps, the busy-bodying interference of peripatetic Princes! You name it and someone somewhere will 'pass the buck'. It seems to me that we have all become used to the idea that the only way to face these great difficulties is to point to someone else. The press has tended to encourage this spirit of confrontation. After all, reporting good news does not sell newspapers. A healthy dispute is what seems to boost the circulation figures, except perhaps in the *Observer*. I hasten to add that I am not blaming the messenger. To do so at this celebration of the *Observer*'s 200th anniversary would be thoroughly ungracious. And the *Observer* was one of the first newspapers to maintain a consistent focus on environmental issues. It is very sad that Geoffrey Lean, its foremost environmental reporter, is not with us today owing to ill health. I wish him as speedy a recovery as possible, because it is journalists of his calibre who make us aware of some of the urgent issues of our time -- and with the use of good English, if I may say so, which makes such a difference as far as I am concerned.

Returning to the theme of our immense environmental problems, it has to be said that the job of finding solutions would be a great deal easier if governments would openly declare what needs to be done. But in the case of the Third World we will first have to create incentives for people to be honest about their difficulties, without fear of imposed solutions. That will involve building a mutual trust and understanding because Third World countries need to be confident that a frank dialogue will not be rewarded with a new set of conditions imposed on them from outside. That would not only be an affront to their sovereign rights, but also a certain way of closing down all dialogue for the future. Without this basic respect for the other person's point of view, the incentives to co-operate are just not there. Bitterness and confrontation grow and solutions become even more remote.

But this must be a two-way process. The taxpayers of the North understandably want assurance that money spent on aid flows is not going to be wasted or stolen by mismanagement and corruption. They need to be confident that everything possible is being done to ensure sound governance for the future. That seems a perfectly fair and reasonable approach to take.

I was encouraged to learn, for instance, that the Group of 7 Summit meeting last year led to a close dialogue between the World Bank, the European Community and Brazil to define a pilot programme for Amazonia. I understand that this is a broad programme put forward by Brazil, including many problems that some people here would think have nothing to do with deforestation. First among them, in my view, is the job of assuring a viable standard of living for the communities now resident in the Amazonian region. This must be based upon sustained management of that great natural asset. It will no doubt include reserve areas as well as new models of harvesting the forest's resources. I look forward very much to my trip to Brazil next month to learn more of the problems and possibilities at first hand.

The reason why I have such a great interest in this community approach is that it is, in my experience, at the community level that most is being done to protect the environment. We can all too hastily get caught up in global negotiations whilst forgetting that people need to be free to pursue sustainable development for themselves. The reconciliation of environmental protection with economic advance essentially comes down to a mass of local problems. These all add up to global issues, but the solutions are local. Providing the right conditions for solutions at the **local** level I would have thought, is the challenge for governments.

The local approach seems to me to be common sense. When people have a right to participate in defining what happens around them, when they have secure tenure to land and when they have a source of credit that is short of usury, they **do** invest in the long term. All communities contain individuals who are naturally entrepreneurial. They organize, co-operate and trade. The result is that they improve their housing, their sanitation systems, their schools and their environments. This happens equally in our own cities as well as those of Africa, China, India and Latin America. In each case the secret is to find the people who really make things happen -- the natural leaders -- and **enable** them, even if that does mean taking a controlled risk with taxpayers' money. Because with the right support and training they are far more effective at getting things done in their own communities than by leaving it up to officials and 'experts', operating from the large metropolitan centres, however well-intentioned they may be. Empowering communities seems to me to be one of the most important keys to fostering a sense of stewardship and community, based on environmental care.

The non-governmental community know this all too well. If you ask our NGO's (Non-governmental Organizations) what they have to show for their efforts, they will often point to local examples carried out despite the difficulties imposed by authorities. In each case, people who want a secure future for their children -- just as we all do -- have to be encouraged to look after the more pressing problems for themselves. To find solutions to problems **they** have identified -- which is what participation implies -- and from which **they** will benefit -- which is what equity implies.

My final point concerns the private or industrial sector, because I believe we are being naive if we think we can achieve a sustainable future without harnessing the best of the corporate world to those ends. Fortunately, there is a growing recognition by people at the top of the most successful businesses of the need for what I can best describe as 'good corporate citizenship'. Society in the 1990's has high expectations of businesses -- not just expectations of their financial performance, but of the whole ethos of their relations with individual communities, wherever they are based or happen to trade.

I would have thought tackling poverty, hunger, homelessness, illiteracy and environmental degradation, wherever it is found in the world, is a true test of a civilized society. No effort to resolve these issues can be truly successful without business playing its part in partnership with government and local communities. Equally, business is able to bring unique skills, resources, technological know-how, determination and, even more importantly, lobbying-power to these issues. It is my personal belief that businesses which ignore the need for action of this kind will not secure their future markets, their customers or their employees.

So, Ladies and Gentlemen, as we move, in 1992, to the international conference on environment and development issues, I do hope the assembled group will concentrate on the themes I have touched upon. A sense of partnership and dialogue that respects sovereign rights, a recognition that poverty is a key factor in environmental destruction, and that the solution to this involves liberating the human spirit and entrepreneurial effort from unnecessary bureaucracy, unacceptable corruption and inequity everywhere.

Many 'ordinary' parents, I suspect, would agree that education is not about social engineering, but about preparing our children as best we can for all the challenges in front of them. This means not only training them for work through the acquisition of knowledge, but also giving them an understanding of themselves and of the deeper meaning of life.

ANNUAL SHAKESPEARE BIRTHDAY LECTURE DELIVERED BY H.R.H. THE PRINCE OF WALES

The Swan Theatre, Stratford-upon-Avon
22nd April 1991

Ladies and Gentlemen,

IT MAY prove to be exceptionally opportune -- in view of what I have to say to you today in this theatre -- that I take off for Brazil as soon as I leave Stratford, probably never to return until found in the last remaining patch of rainforest by a tribe of hunter-gatherer environmentalists ...

Now, I imagine that it is bad enough being asked to deliver the annual Shakespeare lecture if you are one of the many experts on the subject -- a frighteningly large number of whom seem to be gathered in the theatre here this morning. I have no claim to such scholarship and find it hard to decide whether I feel more humble or just downright stupid standing before you today ...

Of one thing at least I am certain. This year you will have a rest from scholarly expertise.

> I am no orator as Brutus is,
> But (as you know me all) a plain blunt man.
> ... And that they know full well
> (- at least I certainly hope they do -)
> That gave me public leave to speak of him.

I have to confess that my acquaintance with Shakespeare began in singularly undistinguished fashion. You have probably already guessed that the 'O' level text we ground our way through at Gordonstoun was *Julius Caesar*. The experience left me largely unmoved. That is perhaps not surprising, since it became only too apparent to me that I was a late developer -- of a particularly virulent kind. It was only quite recently that I re-read the play and appreciated for the first time the fascination of that complex character Brutus, the reluctant revolutionary; the excitement and rhetoric of Anthony's great speeches, and the extraordinary timelessness of Shakespeare's presentation and analysis of riot, revolution, intrigue and internecine strife which is at the heart of the play.

One of the problems, I suspect, was that I failed to realise just what fun Shakespeare could be.

> Brush up your Shakespeare
> Start quoting him now.
> Brush up your Shakespeare
> And the women you will wow.
> Just declaim a few lines from *Othella*
> And they'll think you're a helluva fella.
> If your blonde won't respond when you flatter 'er
> Tell her what Tony told Cleopater-er.
>
> And if still to be shocked she pretends, well
> Just remind her that "All's well that ends well".

Such was the advice given by Cole Porter, that 20th-century master of popular culture, in his musical *Kiss me Kate*. Cole Porter's teasingly affectionate acknowledgement that Shakespeare can actually be fun seems to me to be something which each generation has to discover anew for itself.

All of us who have been fortunate enough to develop an acquaintance with, and love of, Shakespeare -- and that is a thought to which I will return later -- have our favourite plays. One of mine happens to be *Henry V*. This probably has something to do with the fact that it was the first Shakespearean play in which I was able to play a part. As the Duke of Exeter, I was allowed one rather splendid speech at the French Court, but then faded from view, apart from a couple of reappearances on the battlefield at Agincourt and a modest walk-on role in the final scene.

I have seen the play a few times since then. I was spell-bound by Kenneth Branagh's performance at Stratford (how on earth did he manage it at the age of 23?) and I have seen his film of *Henry V* at least three times. Some find it a rather jingoistic play, glorifying war. Certainly there are great speeches of resolute action. But each time I have seen or read the play, it has been the humanity of the King that has moved me most.

> Upon the King! Let us our lives, our souls,
> Our debts, our careful wives,
> Our children and our sins lay on the King!
> We must bear all. O hard condition,
> Twin-born with greatness, subject to the breath
> Of every fool, whose sense no more can feel
> But his own wringing! What infinite heart's ease
> Must Kings neglect, that private men enjoy!
> And what have Kings, that privates have not too,
> Save ceremony, save general ceremony? ...
>
> 'Tis not the balm, the sceptre and the ball,
> The sword, the mace, the crown imperial,
> The intertissued robe of gold and pearl,
> The farced title running 'fore the king,
> The throne he sits on, nor the tide of pomp
> That beats upon the high shore of this world,
> No, not all these, thrice-gorgeous ceremony,
> Not all these, laid in bed majestical,
> Can sleep so soundly as the wretched slave,
> Who with a body fill'd and vacant mind
> Gets him to rest, cramm'd with distressful bread;
> Never sees horrid night, the child of hell,
> But, like a lackey, from the rise to set
> Sweats in the eye of Phoebus and all night
> Sleeps in Elysium; ...

When I re-read this play nearly 20 years after performing in it at school, I found myself wondering in amazement at Shakespeare's insight into the mind of someone born into this kind of royal position. When I was at school I was too young and inexperienced in life to appreciate such subtleties. But now that I have lived life, made mistakes and suffered a bit here and there, I realize how profoundly wise and ageless is Shakespeare's perceptiveness.

Of course, that speech from *Henry V* is not just about the innermost concerns of Kings. It is about the loneliness of high office, the responsibilities and stresses which afflict all those who shoulder great burdens, run industries or schools -- or perhaps nurse invalided relatives.

And, then, what about Henry's speech before Agincourt? Visiting British troops in Saudi Arabia just before Christmas last year, and knowing that a friend of mind was commanding a regiment in the desert, the words that Shakespeare puts into the King's mouth became even more poignant to me. They say everything that ever needs to be said in such circumstances, no matter what age we live in:

> This day is called the Feast of Crispian.
> He that outlives this day and comes safe home
> Will stand a-tiptoe when this day is named
> And rouse him at the name of Crispian.
> He that shall see this day and live t'old age
> Will yearly on the vigil feast his neighbours
> And say 'Tomorrow is Saint Crispian'.
> Then will he strip his sleeve and show his scars
> And say, 'These wounds I had on Crispin's day.'
> Old men forget; yet all shall be forgot,
> But he'll remember, with advantages,
> What feats he did that day. Then shall our names,
> Familiar in his mouth as household words -
> Harry the King, Bedford and Exeter,
> Warwick and Talbot, Salisbury and Gloucester -
> Be in their flowing cups freshly remembered.
> This story shall the good man teach his son,
> And Crispin Crispian shall ne'er go by
> From this day to the ending of the world
> But we in it shall be remembered,
> We few, we happy few, we band of brothers.
> For he today that sheds his blood with me
> Shall be my brother; be he ne'er so vile,
> This day shall gentle his condition.

And gentleman in England now abed
Shall think themselves accursed they were not here,
And hold their manhoods cheap whiles any speaks
That fought with us upon Saint Crispin's day.

One of the unique qualities of Shakespeare -- which has, like every other aspect of his genius, survived almost 400 years -- is his all-encompassing view of mankind. All human life really is there, with an extraordinary range and subtlety of characterization, of historical setting, of place. His understanding of domestic life, of the minds of soldiers and politicians, of the fundamental relationships between men and women was so vast that it remains eternally relevant. Contrast this passage from *Hamlet*:

What a piece of work is a man! How noble in reason,
how infinite in faculty, in form and moving how express
and admirable, in action how like an angel, in
apprehension how like a god -- the beauty of the world,
the paragon of animals!

with this more recent statement from Francis Bacon, proclaimed by the media as the greatest English painter since Turner:

> I think that man now realizes that he is an accident, that he is a completely futile being, that he has to play out the game without reason ... You see, all art has now become completely a game by which man distracts himself; and you may say that it has always been like that, but now it is entirely a game.

Which do you think will ultimately be more relevant?

Time and again in Shakespeare's characters we recognize elements of ourselves. Othello's jealousy, Hamlet's indecision, Macbeth's ambition are all horribly familiar. Shakespeare has that ability to draw characters so universal that we recognize them alive and around us today, every day of our lives.

The evidence shows wonderfully clearly that Shakespeare was a consummate technician and psychologist, with a remarkable ability to understand what makes us all what we are. But it is worth remembering that it is not entirely coincidental that he confronts us so often with such eternal truths, such blunt reminders of the flaws in our own personalities, and of the mess which we so often make of our lives.

His plays are a direct inheritance of the humanism of the Mystery plays, so popular in later Medieval Europe, which deliberately set out to hand on to future generations essential knowledge and experience under the guise of entertainment. No formal education -- just the communication of wisdom through the evocation and study of human emotion, thought and behaviour.

Shakespeare plays a similar game. He has a moral standpoint: his plays helped people to understand themselves, and to recognize the laws of emotion and nature which govern their lives. Listen to Prospero in *The Tempest*:

> ... Our revels now are ended. These our actors,
> As I foretold you, were all spirits, and
> Are melted into air, into thin air;
> And like the baseless fabric of this vision,
> The cloud-capped towers, the gorgeous palaces,
> The solemn temples, the great globe itself,
> Yea, all which it inherit, shall dissolve;
> And, like this insubstantial pageant faded,
> Leave not a rack behind. We are such stuff
> As dreams are made on, and our little life
> Is rounded with a sleep.

Shakespeare holds up a mirror for us to see ourselves and to experience ourselves, so that we gain in the process a more profound understanding of ourselves and others, appreciating right and wrong, and the factors which make us behave as we do.

Art in its broadest sense provides us with the most remarkable access to some of the essential truths about the meaning and significance of life. Poetry and drama are the forms in which, from the most ancient times, human values have been expressed, if not created. In every age of our history, poets and painters, musicians and dramatists have transformed crude fact into human meaning, adding new regions to the kingdom of the imagination.

Artists -- and, again I use the term in its widest possible sense -- have a unique capacity to illustrate, to educate, and to inspire. It is the poet who reveals to us true beauty. Think back, for example, to Enobarbus's glorious description of Cleopatra:

> The barge she sat in, like a burnished throne
> Burned on the water. The poop was beaten gold;
> Purple the sails, and so perfumed that
> The winds were love sick with them. The oars were silver,
> Which to the tune of flutes kept stroke, and made
> The water which they beat to follow faster,
> As amorous of their strokes. For her own person,
> It beggared all description.

In the same way, it is the painter who gives depth to those everyday items so familiar that we fail to appreciate them. It is the pen of the cartoonist or satirist which lays bare the hypocrisy and deceit with which we all, politicians and individuals alike, seek to camouflage our real intentions. Such is the truth and morality which springs from art. Shelley had it right 200 years ago: "Poets are the unacknowledged legislators of the world."

I am one of those who do not believe, as the scientific rationalists seem to, that human consciousness is the product merely of brain processes, or that the cosmos is a huge machine to be examined, experimented with and manipulated by man for his own all-knowing purposes. There is more to mankind, in my view, than a mere mechanical object functioning in a mechanistic world, which has evolved from the clockwork universe of Newton to the computer models now deemed to possess artificial intelligence.

Despite all the dramatic changes that have been wrought by science and technology, and the remarkable benefits they have brought us, there remains deep in the soul of each of us, I believe, a vital metaphysical ingredient which makes life worth living. This awareness of a spiritual dimension greater than, and beyond, the confines of our everyday self, and of a purely superficial perception of the physical world in which we exist, has a particular link to aesthetic experience, and to literature.

Great literature offers one of the keys to understanding these truths, and to understanding ourselves. Shakespeare understood this point very clearly. There is a marvellous, definitive rejection of the rootless, soulless, mechanistic view of man in *The Merchant of Venice*:

The man that hath no music in himself,
Nor is not moved with concord of sweet sounds,
Is fit for treasons, stratigems and spoils;
The motions of his spirit are dull as night
And his affections dark as Erebus:
Let no such man be trusted.

It is our enormous good fortune that the world's greatest playwright -- perhaps the world's greatest poet -- wrote in our own language. The truths he illustrates are universal. In this sense we can read not only a good story into all his plays, but also psychological insights and archetypes with all their engaging interplay. There are also insights into the contemporary political climate, heavily overlaid with symbolism. But, above all, as with all mature art of any civilization, Shakespeare gives us his own version of the journey of the soul from differentiation to unification. Just listen to Lorenzo talking to Jessica in *The Merchant of Venice*:

Sit Jessica - look how the floor of heaven
Is thick inlaid with patens of bright gold.
There's not the smallest orb which thou behold'st
But in his motion like an angel sings,
Still quiring to the young-eyed Cherubins:
Such harmony is in immortal souls,
But whilst this muddy vesture of decay
Doth grossly close it in, we cannot hear it.

Shakespeare's message is the universal, timeless one, yet clad in the garments of his time. He is not just our poet, but the world's. Yet his roots are ours, his language is ours, his culture ours -- brought up in this gentle Warwickshire countryside, educated at the Grammar School in Stratford, baptised and buried in the local parish church.

For us all, roots are important: roots in our landscape and local communities; roots in our cultural and literary heritage; roots in our philosophical and spiritual traditions. If we lose touch with them, if we lose track of where we have come from, we deprive ourselves of a sense of value, a sense of security and all too frequently, a sense of purpose and meaning.

Today's world is changing rapidly; too rapidly, sometimes, for the human psyche to adapt. International barriers are coming down. Economic and political integration are getting ever closer. At the same time peoples all over the world remain as conscious as ever of their national and cultural identities. Look at the fragmentation of the Soviet Union, the resurgence of nationalist sentiment in Central and Eastern Europe, the situation of the long-suffering Kurds -- even the anxieties of many Western Europeans not to allow their national identities to be subsumed in some characterless, grey, multinational bureaucracy.

Hanging onto our cultural roots is one way of preserving those identities, and indeed the stability of our civilizations. Other countries, particularly those with a strong cultural tradition of their own, understand the importance of this and the value of acquainting each new generation with their literary inheritance. In France, the curriculum for all students doing the baccalaureat obliges every student to study a major dramatic work of the 17th century, a philosophical work of the 18th century, a poetical work or novel of the 19th century, and a selection of poetry, novels and drama of the 20th century.

Why is it, then, that we in this country seem to see things differently? There are now several GCSE (General Certificate of Secondary Education) English Literature courses which prescribe no Shakespeare at all. There is at least one A-level English Literature syllabus on which Shakespeare is not compulsory. Thousands of intelligent children leaving school at sixteen have never seen a play of Shakespeare on film or on the stage, and have never been asked to read a single word of any one of his plays. Even the Bank of England has caught the disease, with last week's news that the bard's picture is to be removed from the £20 note!

I find all this difficult to understand. In an age when we are bombarded, perhaps saturated, with instant information of every bewildering kind -- the sort of information which, if we are not careful, can overwhelm and deeply depress us (only to be forgotten a few days later) -- has anyone stopped to consider whether all this actually helps to make us wiser human beings? Wisdom comes through insight, and our greatest poets and literary geniuses are invariably the means by which we can obtain this insight into the workings of the Universe and into the timeless imperatives to which we, as individuals, are subject.

I am not, of course, suggesting that great classical literature and art can be set up as a completely separate alternative to the culture of our times. As a practical man, with practical human concerns, Shakespeare doesn't ask to be canonized, but to live alongside and illuminate the modern realities of life. Look how school groups can respond to live experiences and experimentation! Six-year old children can be enthralled by *Twelfth Night*, slightly older children become frenzied at the sword fights in *Hamlet*. And during school matinees children call out, "Don't do it!" when Romeo is on the point of committing suicide, not knowing that Juliet is still alive.

Shakespeare may be less than fully appreciated in his native land. But he is studied and admired the world over. I shall never forget the number of Danes who came to see *Hamlet* performed at Elsinore three years ago, by the Renaissance Theatre Company when I was also present. Their knowledge of this foreign play was remarkable and it was worth going all the way to Elsinore just to hear the audience's reaction to the statement that -- "Something is rotten in the State of Denmark!"

Whether we realise it or not, Shakespeare is a part of our daily lives. We all shake our heads in despair "more in sorrow than in anger"; all weddings, we hope, are built on "the marriage of true minds"; and gardeners like me throughout the country wonder why even the fullest respect for organic principles produces "things rank and gross in nature" in our flower beds.

It is easy to forget how close we came to losing much of Shakespeare's genius. He made no provision for publication during his lifetime so it is largely his friends and admirers whom we must thank for collecting his writings together after his death. In their first Folio dedicated to his work, Heminges and Condell wrote in their Preface of Shakespeare

> Who, as he was a most happy imitator of Nature was a most gentle expresser of it. His mind and hand went together: And what he thought, he uttered with that easiness that we have scarce received from him a blot in his papers. But it is not our province, who only gather his works, to praise him. It is yours that read him. ... Read him, therefore; and again and again: And if then you do not like him, surely you are in some manifest danger not to understand him.

It ought not to be beyond the ability of our schools and our teachers to protect their pupils from that "manifest danger". For the aids to understanding today are such that it should be easier than ever to ensure that all the young are able to appreciate their cultural inheritance. Just as Peter Schaffer's magnificent film *Armadeus* introduced Mozart's music to millions who had barely a passing acquaintance of it before, so films and practical theatre workshops are there to open a window to Shakespeare for untold numbers of the uninitiated, and to make it comprehensible and contemporary. And here, let me say how much I admire the work in this area of the Royal Shakespeare Company, whose guests we are today, and of the Renaissance Theatre Company of which I am a proud but thoroughly non-acting Patron.

As we move towards a National Curriculum for our schools -- sometimes known as an entitlement curriculum -- I find myself wondering why the students of our schools are not as entitled to Shakespeare as to other parts of the syllabus? Do those who disapprove of Shakespeare, arguing for some extraordinary reason that he is elitist, wish to deprive those not already familiar with his work from acquiring an understanding of it -- or of other great literature?

This marginalising of Shakespeare seems to be symptomatic of a general flight from our great literary heritage. Do we really want to sanction a situation where children are rarely introduced nowadays to the literary masterpieces of bygone ages; where the overwhelming majority leave school without any awareness of Chaucer, Donne, Milton, Pope, Austen, Wordsworth, Keats, Tennyson, Hardy, Dickens ...? Are we all so frightened and cowed by the shadowy 'experts' that we can no longer "screw our courage to the sticking place" and defiantly insist that they are talking unmitigated nonsense? You forget -- I have been through all this before with the architects! I've heard it all over and over again, and it is high time that the bluff of the so-called 'experts' was called. If our newspapers rose to the challenge and conducted a survey amongst their readers, the silent majority might finally be able to say what it really thought on this subject....

I am sure that most teachers would willingly rise to the challenge of introducing their pupils to an experience which, whilst perhaps initially difficult, will be with them for the rest of their lives -- although I am only too aware that there are many teachers who have so despaired of the hostility and indifference of some of the pupils confronting them in their classrooms that they have felt it better to teach them something, rather than nothing at all. Isn't this an area where the National Curriculum should be helping them? I know that the Attainment

Targets for English state that children should be introduced to -- and I quote -- "... some of the works which have been most influential in shaping and refining the English language and its literature e.g. the Authorised Version of the Bible, Wordsworth's poems ... the novels of Austen, the Brontes or Dickens ... some of the works of Shakespeare." This is an encouraging injunction, but I do seriously wonder whether it is enough to counteract what many consider to be an accelerating erosion of serious literary study over the last twenty years.

There are terrible dangers, it seems to me, in so following fashionable trends in education -- trends towards the 'relevant', the exclusively contemporary, the immediately palatable -- that we end up with an entire generation of culturally disinherited young people. I, for one, don't want to see that happen in this country. Nor, I suspect, do countless parents up and down the nation, who probably feel utterly powerless in the face of yet another profession, this time the 'educationists', which I believe has become increasingly out of touch with the true feelings of so-called 'ordinary' people.

Many 'ordinary' parents, I suspect, would agree that education is not about social engineering, but about preparing our children as best we can for all the challenges in front of them. This means not only training them for work through the acquisition of knowledge, but also giving them an understanding of themselves and of the deeper meaning of life. The process is of course complex -- and I think it worth underlining that it is every bit as much the responsibility of parents as of teachers -- not least because it begins at a very early age.

Here in Britain, we seem to get it wrong almost before we have begun. In France, Italy and Belgium every child under 5 receives nursery education from the state. Here, less than half of our children have that right. When they reach primary level, what awaits them? Certainly a great many devoted and committed teachers, many no doubt inspirational, but as often as not, too great an emphasis on the child-centred approach, the open-ended learning situation, and too much stress on process rather than content. Of course, this can engender enthusiasm and interest in the classroom, but seems correspondingly less likely to instil fundamental standards of accuracy in the basic skills.

It is almost incredible that in Shakespeare's land one child in seven leaves primary school functionally illiterate. Moreover, it appears to be an increasingly common impression that standards of handwriting, spelling, punctuation and numeracy are not at all what they should be. In most schools children are deemed incapable of learning foreign languages before the age of 11 -- yet by the age of 14 half of them have given it up. As if that wasn't enough, present indications are that after the age of 14 children will not be required by the National Curriculum to study any aesthetic subject.

Perhaps most alarming of all, only one-third of our 16-18 year olds are still in full-time education. In France the figure is 66%, Japan 77%, the United States 79%, the Netherlands 77%. Forty per cent of our children leave full-time schooling with no significant educational qualifications at all.

On reflection, it is not all that surprising that so many leave school as soon as they can. Sixth-form education is, after all, geared mainly to preparing pupils for universities, polytechnics or other forms of further education. This inevitably frightens off those who are less academically-minded, if it does not simply disqualify those who would like to do so, from staying on.

Meanwhile, those of our pupils who do stay on for the sixth-form study three, or at most four, subjects. The advantage of such specialization is that those subjects tend to be covered in a depth which gives our undergraduates a strong start when they begin their university studies. The disadvantage is that they often miss out on education in a whole range of other subjects. Are we sure that mathematicians do not need to learn to write English, or speak foreign languages? Or that our historians can survive without an understanding of economics and philosophy? It is almost unknown in other countries (including Scotland, where the advantages of a broader education seem to be much better understood) for there to be this exclusive concentration on such a limited range of subjects.

It would be encouraging to think that an attractive programme of vocational training was available for the large numbers of our young people coming out of full-time education at sixteen. In Germany there is virtually no labour market for 16-18 year olds outside the apprentice system. Moreover, employers are legally obliged to give *all* young adults at least one day off a week for off-the-job training.

Here at home it is a sadder story. Most of those who leave school the moment they can, go straight on to the labour market -- or more depressingly, and I have seen it often enough -- onto the register of unemployed. What a way to begin adult life! Only now are we coming to terms with the price we have paid for allowing the apprenticeship system to wither away. Only now are we putting in place arrangements to give our young people the vocational qualifications which they -- and the country -- need.

It is heartening that commercial firms are increasingly involved in such training schemes, and are partners with government in the Training and Enterprise Councils set up two years ago. But, as a nation, we have been appallingly slow in bridging the huge gulf between the start we give our young people and the preparation for work which they receive in other countries. We have also been slow to see the disadvantages of forcing our children to choose between either an academic education or a technical, vocational one -- a divisive practice almost unknown in other countries. What worries me so much is how we are going to survive in the Europe of 1992 and beyond shackled with such manifest handicaps.

We must have missed a few tricks when, at the beginning of the last century, Napoleon set up the Lycée system in France together with the prestigious state-run Grandes Écoles accessible to anyone able to satisfy the rigorous entry qualifications. In Prussia Prince William von Humboldt was doing the same thing with the Gymnasien. We persevered, instead, with our reliance on the ancient universities and public schools as centres of excellence.

In our times education has suffered badly from the process of lurching from one set of policy initiatives to another, as governments change, and a seemingly endless squeeze on resources. The result -- sadly, at a time when education faces greater challenges than ever before -- has been a major onset of innovation fatigue, a teaching force which invariably feels underpaid and demoralised, with inadequate attention being paid to their accommodation and equipment needs.

Encouragingly, there is now a greater concensus perhaps than ever before that education is the number one priority for the future. The overall concept of a National Curriculum seems to be agreed by all political parties -- and most teachers. So too, is the need to do something about the education -- and training -- of our 16-18 year olds. There is talk of the establishment of a new National Commission to look into educational opportunities for *all*. And last week's announcement of a new pay review body for the teachers could go a long way towards encouraging more first-rate people to choose teaching as a career. The prospects for getting things right may therefore be better than they have been for a long time.

Let us, therefore, Ladies and Gentlemen, grasp this opportunity and resist the temptation to deny the cultural heritage of our country to so many young people simply because of expediency or because of a mistaken utilitarian approach. We live in an age obsessed with the tangible, with discernible results and with that which is measurable. While applauding the stress that has to be placed on the technical, the practical, the vocational and the commercially viable, I would like to stress, again, that I believe that education is more than just training. After all, there is little point in becoming technically competent if at the same time we become culturally inept.

In pleading for a restoration of sanity, I have to admit to a feeling of profound sadness that a very great deal of damage has already been done; and that in the unlikely event of anyone taking serious notice of what is said by those of us who care deeply about the value of a grounding in our greatest literature, it will take far too long to put things back on course. I feel an overwhelming shame that in a country like Britain we should have allowed such a short-sighted approach to predominate. As Parolles says in *All's well that ends well* --

> I shall lose my life for want of language.

If we fail to change the present situation, from what roots shall we produce our future poets, playwrights and authors? What, then, will become of

> ... This royal throne of Kings, this sceptred isle,
> This earth of majesty, this seat of Mars,
> This other Eden, demi-paradise,
> This fortress built by nature for herself
> Against infection and the hand of war,
> This happy breed of men, this little world,
> This precious stone set in the silver sea,
> Which serves it in the office of a wall,
> Or as a moat defensive to a house,
> Against the envy of less happier lands;
> This blessed plot, this earth, this realm, this England,
> This nurse, this teeming womb of royal kings,
> Feared by their breed and famous by their birth?

I don't want my children -- or anybody else's -- to be deprived of Shakespeare, or of the other life-enhancing elements which I have suggested should be part of the schooling entitlement of all the children of this country. And I don't want our future generations to be the poor relations in a Europe in which there will be less and less room for those who can't keep up. But I fear that these are real dangers if we evade those key questions about the nature and purpose of education which I have touched on today, and if we fail to give our schools and our teachers the resources, and the philosophical framework, they need in order to produce the right results.

I do not expect you to agree with me, but I believe that the most urgent need for western man is to rediscover that divine element in his being, without which there never can be any possible hope or meaning to our existence in the Earthly realm..

LECTURE BY H.R.H. THE PRINCE OF WALES, AS PATRON, TO THE ROYAL COLLEGE OF PSYCHIATRISTS

Brighton, Friday 5th July, 1991

LITTLE DID I think when I accepted the invitation to become the Patron of your College that you would finally catch up with me in your 150th year by strapping me to a lectern and forcing yourselves to listen to me. However, I can only assume that if your professional reputation is anything to go by I should at least be guaranteed the best audience I have ever had!

Personally, I think I need my head examined for coming all the way to Brighton merely to reveal my lamentable ignorance about the complex problems with which you have to deal in your professional lives. By the time I have finished this morning I dare say it shouldn't be too difficult to diagnose what is wrong with me, and no doubt you will then all argue furiously over the course of treatment to be prescribed. My guess is that you will recommend complete rest for another two weeks accompanied by a total abstinence from stress-inducing speeches....!

Talking of stress-inducing speeches, I am afraid I don't have a very good record when it comes to the 150th anniversaries of professional bodies. The British Medical Association and then the Royal Institute of British Architects discovered, too late, the folly of their invitation to such an unreliable speaker! I can only imagine you have invited me under the delusion that you can actually cure me! Whatever the case, please know that I come here today as someone who is honoured to be your Patron, who brings you heartfelt congratulations on the achievement of such a distinguished anniversary and who makes no pretence of speaking in any other capacity than as a layman. But you must foregive me if I speak from time to time from the heart -- it is a congenital defect! In this spirit I want you to know how much I sympathise with you in what must be, at times, a literally soul-destroying task. As a profession your calling is to try to bring a measure of healing and comfort to the mental anguish and suffering of countless numbers of people. And yet you have to operate in an environment which I suspect most people who consider themselves sane and "normal" (whatever that is!) prefer to shun or to make jokes about. Not only that, but you are also working within the confines of current society, whose attitude and outlook must necessarily colour your approach.

I know that there have many debates both within and without psychiatry as to what is a helpful definition of mental health, but as yet no proposal has won general agreement. I can imagine, therefore, that psychiatrists are often left with having to respond to people with acutely disturbed behaviour and to try to offer treatment that will lessen or eliminate the extreme behaviour presented -- for the person and those around them.

I know, too, of the countless debates there have been within the profession regarding the nature of the task you have set yourselves in the last 150 years -- in particular the arguments about psychotherapy and psychiatry, the latter having grown out of a branch of general medicine and which therefore is concerned with finding a physical basis for the major psychiatric disorders.

A hundred and fifty years ago, people had very limited, but nevertheless clear and important, definitions of madness. They had little idea or understanding of the causes but were quite clear that madness was to do with unacceptable behaviour. The term described certain forms of violence, and unacceptable responses to social situations. It constituted a failure to relate to other human beings. In some respects this is a definition from which we have not advanced, but during that time generations of psychiatrists have made major progress towards understanding and treating mental illness. It is, therefore, perhaps disappointing that society's understanding and acceptance of mental illness has developed so little during the same period, and that there is still somewhat of a social stigma attached to it.

A stigma is 'a distinguishing mark of social disgrace', and ultimately comes from a Greek word meaning 'to tattoo'. This appropriately conveys the image, for the mentally ill person, of being branded: perhaps the one who causes a disturbance on the underground, or someone whose unacceptable behaviour embarrasses family and friends. The quiet, unobtrusive sufferer from depression understandably fears being tarred with the same brush. As a result he dares not admit to symptoms and so does not receive treatment until he or she has suffered greatly for an unnecessarily long time. This stigma makes the whole of life even more difficult for both the mentally ill and the mentally handicapped; it affects the patients themselves, their relatives and all who deal with them. This tends to include mental health professionals, who themselves can become subtly tainted.

I know that the Royal College of Psychiatrists aims to try to remove this stigma altogether and is working to lessen its effect. Providing the facts for the general public about the different mental illnesses is helpful, and efforts in public education such as the College's 'Beat Depression' campaign can certainly help. The media obviously have an important part to play in the process and there are shining examples of what can be done, such as the series of articles by Marjorie Wallace in *The Times* which not only laid the foundation of contemporary understanding of schizophrenia, but also led directly to the formation of a charity called SANE, of which I am Patron. As Professor Anthony Clare said in his keynote speech two weeks ago, at the start of your celebrations, "What SANE has done is to strip back the curtains surrounding mental illness, so that the condition is no longer so mystifying. As a result sufferers and families no longer need to feel so neglected and isolated."

There are, it has to be said, sections of the media which do not take such an enlightened view and (perhaps reflecting the views and prejudices of their readers) will go to great lengths to avoid any serious discussion of mental illness. I believe that the difficulty sufferers have in talking about their illness and treatment, and the secrecy surrounding it, gives an added responsibility to professionals like yourselves to speak up, and in terms that everyone can understand. Heart by-pass operations and transplant surgery attract enormous interest, and there is no shortage of ex-patients to testify to the success of the techniques. But disorders such as severe depression and schizophrenia are largely ignored and opportunities for us all to learn anything about their nature and treatment are virtually non-existent.

This same taboo on the public discussion of what are, after all, common illnesses has led, I believe, to a general undervaluing of the work of psychiatrists. Not unnaturally, the brilliant work of our best surgeons attracts a certain sort of glamour. We marvel at, and are grateful for, their successes and share their sorrow when a patient cannot be saved. But psychiatry remains largely unsung -- perhaps because it is also, inevitably, unseen. Its triumphs are, almost by definition, private, and invisible to the public eye. When there are significant failures how often does anyone register the impact they have on the psychiatrists who have done their best? On the contrary, the public perception is all too often negative, driven by the same stigma which attaches to their patients and, quite possibly, to people who are rash enough to make speeches about the subject!

It is sad that society does not generally seem to recognize what it asks of its psychiatrists. Of all the areas of specialist medicine, you cover perhaps the broadest range of disorders, only outdone by the G.P., who also has a key role in the identification and treatment of mental illness. You certainly deal with what is by far the most complex organ in the body. In the absence of anyone else, we would like you to solve all the problems of society. We confront you with the most complex problems, part biological, part psychological, part social and part spiritual, and expect you to unravel them, treat all the parts that belong to psychiatry and at the same time somehow make better all the parts that don't belong to psychiatry.

I am sure it would be helpful if more people understood that a psychiatrist's first problem is to decide how to reach out to a patient, how to make them feel understood, cared for, and safe. Frequently, patients are frightened, not only by their pain, suffering or madness, but also by the image of psychiatry which they may have gained from films or other highly biased sources. I am told that a recent film *The Silence of theLambs* portrays psychiatrists in a quite terrifying manner, which is no doubt a help at the box office, but is none at all to the psychiatrists -- or to those in need of their help.

In our contemporary society there is every incentive to believe that suffering can be banished, avoided or at worst postponed. Psychiatrists have to confront the evidence to the contrary every single day. Just being with a patient who is frightened or frightening must be incredibly difficult and takes immense courage and dedication; the human contact can awaken shadows in the doctor's own psyche, testing that inner strength which has the most profound influence on the patient. To listen and share in someone's pain takes great bravery and it deserves recognition.

In a day's work psychiatrists and psychotherapists will doubtless hear many dark and terrible stories; of loneliness, isolation, poverty and bereavement.

Despite the best efforts of social services, and other caring agencies, children do suffer at the hands of their parents, guardians or other adults. Physical and mental abuse are not uncommon and tend to be perpetuated from one generation to the next. Other children and adults suffer not through the deliberate will of others, but through misfortune, accident, bereavement or other crisis.

Many people are somehow able to redirect this neurotic energy into creativity, perhaps at work, or through various forms of artistic expression, or in spiritual understanding and healing. But for reasons that you and your colleagues are only slowly unravelling there are also people for whom suffering leads to pain, anxiety, depression, drug buse and other forms of mental illness.

Between these two groups are a great many other people who respond to medication, and yet at the same time are influenced by the amount of stress or suffering to which they are exposed. I am told that before modern drugs were available patients with schizophrenia were routinely admitted to hospital and for some of them their symptoms would be ameliorated by providing a structured, peaceful and caring environment. Similarly, it is now known that schizophrenia patients receiving medication need more medication if they are in a family environment which is highly stressed and less in a family which is supportive, and yet accepting, and where there is understanding of the illness.

As I said at the beginning of my lecture, it is not surprising that there has been a lot of discussion about the relative merits of the biological and psychosocial approaches to problems of the psyche. One school of thought claims that mental illness is in the last resort a physical disorder, to be treated by physical means. New drugs make this a powerful and effective approach, which has certainly led to dramatic relief of symptoms and greatly reduced periods of hospitalization. At the same time the power of the technique is such that a psychiatrist faced with a distressed or unhappy person, and probably in a crisis situation, may have to resort to a "chemical cosh" too readily, in order to calm someone quickly -- substituting drugs (which can lead to dependence) for the time and understanding which could conceivably rescue the patient from his predicament.

The other school of thought believes, as you all know better than I, that mental illness is primarily a behavioural malaise, to be treated by methods appropriate to such a disorder. It uses drugs and physical techniques as sparingly as possible, and relies on reaching a close rapport with the patient, helping him or her by psychological analysis in depth to integrate apparently conflicting emotional drives. This view, too, has its undeniable quota of success, but is difficult to apply on a large scale, if only because of the prohibitive cost in time and medical manpower.

Having made my own views on over-reliance on medication known to the British Medical Association some years ago, and having spent some time since then in encouraging what I prefer to call complementary practice, it will not surprise you to hear that I am concerned, for what it is worth, that the psychological approach to mental illness should not be forgotten or discounted.

I know that this College recommends the lowest possible dosage of drugs and encourages the use, wherever possible, of psychological techniques, but all the enquiries I have been able to make have suggested that the training of psychiatrists is heavily weighted towards the medical approach. This may be a reflection of a society which some people would say is overly materialistic, with the emphasis too much on doing and changing, and not enough on being and accepting. The power of the medical techniques is undeniable. They have brought real benefits and no one would wish to deny that. But I would have thought that over-emphasis on drugs can also enable us as a society to lose sight of problems which have their roots in the way we treat each other.

A teenager with hallucinations and strange beliefs may be diagnosed as schizophrenic and be provided with the extensive help and support he or she needs. But another similar teenager may have other serious difficulties -- perhaps an inability to form stable relationships, a tendency to violence or to take overdose during outbursts of uncontrollable rage. Both teenagers need care. The schizophrenic fits neatly into the medical model, whilst the other may be labelled as 'delinquent' or assessed as having a personality disorder. Both conditions are treatable and both require a great deal of time and resources, not only from psychiatrists. One is understandable in terms of illness, the other only in much broader terms, which may involve facing unpleasant realities about our society. No doubt there are people who would say that the patient with a personality problem is not the concern of the psychiatrist. But without proper help and direction such adolescents may go on to deprive and, perhaps, even abuse their own children.

The medically trained psychiatrist could be forgiven for feeling at a loss when faced with a disturbing and frightening young person who neither needs or responds to medication. I believe there is a need for training which emphasizes to psychiatrists that there **will** be times when they will feel overwhelmed when faced with people who have suffered greatly; that there **will** be times when it is important to remain with and be with and comfort such a person in their suffering. Psychiatrists rightly emphasize the importance of communicating clearly and skilfully, and I welcome the growing importance being given to listening and counselling skills in all branches of medicine. Sometimes there is a need for doing, but equally there are times for being with, for waiting, for being patient and for allowing spiritual healing to occur. There is a sense, too, in which suffering, if handled sensitively, can be transmuted into a positively redeeming process. I was talking recently to the wife of a Church of Scotland minister who told me that as often as not she and her husband are left to pick up the pieces with people who have failed to respond to psychiatric treatment. She told me that she has only witnessed a true transformation in such people when they finally discover within themselves that transfiguring dimension we define (or perhaps I should say that some of us define!) as God. Above all, perhaps, students need to be taught that growth and healing are natural processes. Science can accelerate them, but it can also retard or prevent them.

Ladies and Gentlemen, I was interested to observe that the motto of your College is "Let wisdom guide". For what it is worth, I believe we need to be reminded occasionally that wisdom has a far more profound meaning than just the acquisition of knowledge in the modern scientific-material sense. Should we not be asking ourselves pretty carefully where scientific materialism has been leading us -- and, indeed, what kind of society it has been creating? Is there not an imbalance that needs correcting; an abandoned element that requires rehabilitation? It is perhaps worth recalling that Jung himself told one of his associates that he did not want anybody to be "Jungian". "I want people above all to be themselves. As for 'isms', they are the viruses of our day, and responsible for greater disasters than any medieval plague or pest has ever been. Should I be found one day only to have created another 'ism' then I will have failed in all I tried to do."

At the risk of being controversial, (which at least has the advantage of providing a useful source of conversation over lunch!) I would like to pose a few thoughts to you.

In Ancient Greece, sickness of the soul or psyche, needed not the care of ancient medicine or a physician, but exclusively a god or saviour named Asclepius. The reason for this was that classical man saw sickness as the effect of a divine action, which could be cured only by a god or another divine action. Thus a clear form of homeopathy was practised, where the divine sickness was cast out by divine remedy. "When the sickness is vested with such dignity, it has the inestimable advantage that it can be vested with healing power." Thus said C.A. Meier in his *Healing Dream and Ritual.*

Such explanations, of course, run totally counter to 'modern' explanations of mental illness. The modernist will doubtless accuse the proponents of theocentric views of wanting to tip psychiatry back into the dark ages, and bring back ghouls and ghosts and other irrational explanations that muddy our scientific understanding. But perhaps, then, we can ask for an explanation as to how and why such illness **does** arise? Although it may be categorized and its manifestations damped down, I would suggest it is very hard to explain its intrinsic cause.

Is it not because the irrational forces of the universe have been ignored so completely for so long that they can come with such power into the lives of people who have no conception of what is happening? Without experienced people who can work in those worlds, containment, transformation and healing are surely very difficult.

It seems to me that the meaning that illness has for us is, to a large extent, conditioned by our view about the purpose and goal of the life we are given on this planet. In other words, for the materialist, enlightened self-interest would lead us to see illness as of no value with no meaning, whereas someone with a religious view of Creation will need to think about it in a much larger frame than merely the restriction of the individual's ability to do all that he or she could. If wisdom is to be your guide then Shakespeare makes a few salient points when Macbeth speaks to the doctor about Lady Macbeth, thus --

> Canst thou not minister to a mind diseased,
> Pluck from the memory a rooted sorrow,
> Raze out the written troubles of the brain,
> And with somer sweet oblivious antidote
> Cleanse the stuffed bosom of that perilous stuff
> which weighs upon the heart?

The conclusion of the matter was "more needs she the divine than the physician". I do not expect you to agree with me, but I believe that the most urgent need for Western man is to rediscover that divine element in his being, without which there never can be any possible hope or meaning to our existence in this Earthly realm. As Wordsworth wrote with such profound insight --

> And I have felt
> A presence that disturbs me with the joy
> Of elevated thoughts: a sense sublime
> Of something far more deeply interfused,
> Whose dwelling is the light of setting suns
> And the round Ocean and the living air,
> And the blue sky and in the mind of man;
> A motion and a spirit that impels
> All thinking things, all objects of all thought,
> and rolls through all things.

At the heart of many religious, psychological and psychiatric writings is a recognition of the importance of the way in which all the members of our society are inter-connected and inter-dependent, and the need to look at the whole person in the whole society. This, of course, runs directly contrary to our natural instinct to attempt to deal with the complexities of contemporary life by breaking it down into different components. Yet experience shows that if we do not address the whole of a person's needs within the whole of the society in which that person lives, treatment will fail.

I do believe that we are in danger of cutting ourselves off into a world that recognizes only mind and body. But in the treatment of mental illness we must surely recognize the importance of understanding and respecting the culture and beliefs of the individuals concerned and of those close to them. When -- as is too often the case in our generation -- there seem to be no beliefs, but simply a spiritual vacuum, there are no foundations on which to build an acceptance of our own weakness, respect for the unique worth of others, and a reconciliation between those classed as mentally ill and the society in which we must all live.

To take just one example, I believe that one of the conditions most commonly encountered by psychiatrists is despression and anxiety. One of the main causes seems to be the lack of acceptance of suffering in a society which focuses on immediate gratification. We find it hard to accept that there is a need to adapt to loss, and to grieve, and we are intolerant of people who are emotionally distressed. Often their distress is made worse because they do not have the inner resources and spiritual development which would enable them to see that there **is** a meaning beyond themselves.

Treating the whole person within the whole society should perhaps be easier to achieve under the policy of community-based care, with local services designed to help people live as fully and productively as possible, despite their problems or disabilities. I know there are problems and challenges in making the new system work properly, but it does seem that the debate about whether community-based services (in which the role of the hospital is clearly defined) are right in principle, is over. The challenge now is to put those locally-based services in place in **every district**, in keeping with the need for them.

At this point and at the risk of repeating what you already know only too well, it may be worth reminding ourselves of the scale of the problem of mental illness. Quite apart from the cost in terms of human misery, the Mental Health Foundation has calculated that in 1989 no fewer than 71 million working days were lost in the United Kingdom because of mental illness; this represented 17% of all sickness absences from work, and cost this country nearly four billion pounds in lost working days. Other research has shown that in every thousand people, 250 will suffer from a diagnosable mental illness. Of those 250, 17 will go to a psychiatrist and 6 will subsequently enter hospital. That is perhaps a salutary reminder of how much larger the problem is than even you encounter, and I have no doubt at all that some of those you do not see are just as ill as those you do.

But what sort of service do the mentally ill **want**, what do their relatives want? As you know, most want to live at home, to live their separate lives as far as possible like the rest of society. Patients tell me that they do not wish to go to hospital, and yet relatives tell the most awful stories of the deprivation, suffering and terror that they endure in trying to help their loved ones through their illness at home. It seems to me that if community-based care is really going to provide proper support we will need to find ways of giving greater strength, solidity and dependability to local services. But there must also be proper provision for those patients whose overriding need is for refuge and asylum. There will always be people who need a place of sanctuary where they can work through their pain and suffering, with professional support available 24 hours a day, and learn to adjust to their illness and all that it means in terms of loss of ability and potential. To recognize this would be a useful step forward in national policy.

I realize how difficult it must be to make such a complex and far-reaching change in the system as the current move to a community-based service. Though the mental hospitals could be stultifying and disabling, they must have been easier to manage than a network of smaller, sometimes almost invisible, local services. Developing and co-ordinating all these different community services is difficult, too, in part because many of the critical variables are outside the direct control of mental health professionals, planners or managers. Housing, for example, is a vital ingredient which regrettably is often lacking at present, causing all sorts of problems for individuals and for those who are trying to provide the service. It must be very depressing and de-motivating for psychiatrists to do their best for their patients and then be unable to discharge them to decent housing and the prospect of work. At the moment I know there are times when some of you have to discharge patients into poor accommodation, without supervision, often in a deprived area, and without the prospect of a worthwhile occupation, in the certain knowledge that this is going to aggravate their illnesses and result in their return to hospital. Clearly we need to forge new partnerships, not only between health and social services, but also involving housing authorities and housing associations.

What is also frustrating is how confusing the reports on all this tend to be. No one seems to know on a national basis what is really happening to people being diverted or discharged from mental hospitals. Studies of those resettled from hospital are generally very encouraging, but we know much less about those who have fallen through the cracks and those who might have been hospitalized in a previous era. I believe there is a need to monitor what is happening more carefully in order to get the national picture into focus. As a BBC 'Panorama' programme earlier this week illustrated, there are undoubtedly people appearing in the accident departments, the courts and the prisons who represent the casualties from current policies.

Another group with a major contribution to make is the General Practitioners. Very many people with psychological symptoms consult their family doctor, but in about half of all cases the G.P. does not recognize the condition as a psychiatric disorder, and even where the condition is regarded as psychiatric it may go untended. This is hardly surprising as it is still possible to enter general practice as a Principal with as little as eight weeks of experience of studying psychiatry. I would have thought that there was an urgent need for more training for G.P.'s in psychiatry, both in the identification of mental illnesses and in their effective treatment. Since I am about to become next year's President of the

Royal College of General Practitioners (they need their heads examined as well!), I was interested to learn about an exciting development in community psychiatry which aims to foster closer working ties between these two groups of professionals. The Liaison in Community Psychiatry Programme (known as LINC-UP) begins with a nation-wide survey of all psychiatrists at this conference, and I hope you will all be able to give it your support.

Another area which I hope you will support and encourage is the perhaps somewhat undervalued task of research. This country has a proud reputation in this area, and I know that biological researchers in psychiatry and allied fields are currently beginning to make significant inroads into our understanding of the functioning of the brain. Of course such research is expensive, and last month SANE asked me to launch an appeal to enable the founding of an International Schizophrenia Research Centre in this country. It was the most wonderful start to be able to announce immediately that no less than one and three-quarter million pounds has been pledged to the Centre by King Fahd of Saudi Arabia. The task is now to match this most generous contribution from other sources.

Ladies and Gentlemen, I would like to end by suggesting that any vision of a better future for the people who are afflicted by mental illness must have its roots in a better understanding of mind and body, and in values that go far beyond the material. We will build a better future for the mentally ill because we know what "better" means, and it means radical change in society's assumptions.

It is terrible to have made you sit here for so long (you will all end up with bad backs before I've finished!) but there are just three main points that I would like to leave with you. Firstly, my encouragement and admiration for your intensely difficult, undervalued work with the large group of people who bear the stigma of mental illness.

Secondly, it is clear that the current national and international policies in psychiatry are moving firmly away from the large closed institutions. That is understandable but we still need places of sanctuary **and** we must make community care work. There **are** now good models of success; projects where community care is working really well. But we have a long way to go before those models of excellence are the universal pattern. That is the challenge in our generation.

Finally, my feeling that there is a need for greater recognition, even among such an enlightened group as yourselves, that mental and physical health are not simply about medical repairs. We are **not** just machines, whatever modern science may claim is the case on the evidence of what is purely visible and tangible in this world. Mental and physical health also have a spiritual base. Caring for people who are ill, restoring them to health when that is possible, and comforting them always, even when it is not, are spiritual tasks. Training people for your profession and maintaining your professional skills are not simply about understanding and administering the latest drugs but about therapy; in the original Greek sense of healing -- physical, mental and spiritual, and also about wisdom, in the ancient sense of understanding the true nature of our our existence enabling those who are "seeing through a glass darkly" then to see face to face. If you lose that foundation as a profession, I believe there is a danger you will ultimately lose your way.